> To Talisha

It Worked for Me
Tips for Raising Millennial Daughters

Thank you so much!

Love,
Mom

Monique Young
Hempstead, New York

Copyright © 2017 Monique Young. All rights reserved. No part of this publication may be reproduced, stored in or introduced into a retrieval system, or transmitted, in any form or by any means (electronic, mechanical, photocopying, recording or otherwise), without the prior written permission of the copyright owner.

The scanning, uploading, and distribution of this book via the Internet or any other means without the authorization of the publisher are illegal and punishable by law. Please purchase only authorized electronic editions and do not participate in or encourage electronic piracy of copyrighted materials. Your support of the author's rights is appreciated.

Limits of Liability ~ Disclaimer
The author and publisher shall not be liable for your misuse of this material. This book is strictly for informational and educational purposes. The author and publisher do not guarantee that anyone following these techniques, suggestions, tips, ideas, or strategies will become successful. The author and publisher shall have neither liability nor responsibility to anyone concerning any loss or damage caused, or alleged to be caused, directly or indirectly by the information contained in this book.

Cover Design: Okomota
Editing-Interior Layout: The Self-Publishing Maven
Formatting: Istvan Szabo, Ifj.
Photography: Romee Gooden
Stylist: Daleha

ISBN: 978-0-9993044-0-2
ISBN-10:0-9993044-0-2
Printed in the United States of America

www.mommamonique.com

It Worked for Me

Tips for Raising Millennial Daughters

Monique Young

APPRECIATION

I thank God, who is truly the head of my life. Through him is where all of my blessings flow.

Acknowledgements

To my husband John I have loved you since 1986. Yes, I have 30 years with the same man by my side loving me through all of our moments. You are my rock and without you where would I be? You have been so patient, kind and committed! I could not have been blessed with a better hubby I love you, John Young, you rock!

My sisters Annemarie, Carol, Belinda, Rhonda and my sister in love Alisa. You all have been my support for so long and my right hand. I love you all, and my journey would not have been the same without you.

My big brother Donnell, your silence has been golden all these years (laughing out loud family joke). You have always inspired and protected me, and I will love you forever. Larry and Dwayne thanks for being my brothers in love. Larry, you always make sure I stay smelling good. Dwayne, you love my sister and my family like we are yours and I appreciate you for that. To my little brother Randy, you are the best our father could have made, keep your head up big teddy bear I love you.

My mother in love, Joyce you are the Matriarch of this family and you wear that crown well. Thank you for praying for us and never prying in our marriage, which is a gift that all wives treasure. I love you Grammy for being you, my loving daughters and giving me a great man for a husband.

Marilyn, Sabrina, and Tara what can I say, you ladies have been everything, and I appreciate all that you have done in helping me carry my vision and never letting it die. I love you so much.

My Sistah-Friends, the ones who God hand-picked for me, Angela, Butter, Clara, Kim, Lydia, Margo, Melvina, Norma, Shawanda, Stacie, Stacy & Vernessa. I appreciate every little thing about you, and I would never be me without you. You women make my day-to-day life easier with a phone call or sit down and are always there when needed. I love you, ladies! I have to shout out my girl Regina Ravenell-Carr from the babysitter referral to the publisher you have been dead on I appreciate you girl!

Thank you God for the blessing of my Grandson John-Sekou named for both of his grandpa's and born on both of their birthdays, this was ordained. I realized that I was supposed to be a grandmother to a wonderful baby boy as I have so much to share with him I cannot wait to write about that journey. Jahnique and Hussein, thanks for openly sharing him as I love him so.

Since I started writing this book, two of my good girlfriends received a diagnosis of Stage I Breast Cancer. They have fought, won, and to God be the glory. Love you Alicia and Stacy you got the Victory! Your journey encouraged me to do all the things my heart desired! I want you to know that we will embrace our Jubilee together. 50 is our year, the year when we are going to take back all the devil stole from us!

Love You All!
Monique

Dedication

I dedicate this book to my girls Jeanette, Jahnique, Jorri, and Jalena. Each one of you is unique and special in your own way, and you have bought unexplainable joy to my life. I hope you laugh, cry and most of all be blessed by my testimony. Thank you God for the blessing of my girls, I always wanted a son, but I realized now my charge was to raise young women that would be strong, kind, independent, and beautiful and God fearing. We are still a work in progress, but we are working on our daily walk, and I pray you are encouraged.

Contents

Introduction 1
Part One For My Girls! 3
   Letter to My Newborn 5
   Sorry You Could Not Interview Your Father 19
Part Two For Us Who Have Girls 27
   The Early Years 28
   A Teenager, Who Are You? 37
   60 Seconds of Confession 47
   Dream Big Fear Little 53
   You Are Not Your Skin 60
   Hold Up, Wait a Minute! 66
   You're Gay, But We're Okay 70
   Don't Touch Me! 78
   My Sister's Keeper 85
   Don't Let Your Tongue Be a Taser 100
   Dating – Laughing Out Loud 105
Part Three For Girls and Women in General – What Worked For Me In Life 111
   God Is Important 113
   Why Did She Have To Die? 118
   Traditions vs. Yokes 126
Final Thoughts 130

INTRODUCTION

Parenting can go from exciting to rewarding to stressful at times. Let's face it; we are raising a new generation with new ideas, ideals, and vision. What we may want for them is not necessarily, what they want for themselves, thus, the present generation of *the millennial*.

Known as the peculiar generation in their way of thinking and being, they are the biggest generation of people grossing 80 million in the United States. However, they seem to be the most complex of the generations. As parents we see certain characteristics or states of being like bored, detached, entitled, explorative, outspoken, and passionate, just to name a few. I am blessed to birth four daughters, who now range in age from 15 to 29, and have taught me many lessons on being a mother. From my constant prayers for my purpose, God gave the idea to share our journey and said to me, "Share Your Thoughts Concerning Daughters."

It is my hope from the first chapter to the last that I can give you food for thought that can be used as a reference in one of life's many unpredictable moments.

From the letters I wrote to each of them when born, to working with through the teenage years, virginity, dating, and the list goes on, I pray that this book will serve as a reference guide in raising your daughter or, you will gift a young lady as she prepares for her next phase of life.

To many, I am known as Momma Monique, the woman with the four daughters. I am often asked questions related to all the above subjects I shared. Am I a perfect parent? No, but I believe we should share our experiences to give others the learning curve to life's challenges.

This book is split up into three parts and written in true Momma Monique voice. *Part One* I am writing directly to my daughters because they are the reason why I have a platform to speak freely about parenting. *Part Two*, to those parents who are raising teenagers and grooming their millennial adult children. I am taking a trip down memory lane and sharing tips for the millennial mother who is raising a young girl. *Part Three* is for women in general who want some simple tips that have worked for me throughout my life.

Here is a brief introduction of my cast. There is my partner in crime, my ride or die, also called my boo, my husband, John. We have our girls Jeanette (29), Jahnique (26), Jorri (20), and Jalena (15). They are as different as they come and the same when it comes to loving each other. Read on to learn about them. I ask you to open your mind and heart as you learn a few tips on what has "Worked for Me!"

PART ONE
FOR MY GIRLS!

It Worked for Me...

For each daughter, I wrote a letter as a way of connecting with her from birth and gave it to them when they were older. The goal was for them to know how I felt the day they were born and create a birth stamp which documented what I felt, as well as saw, the moment I laid eyes on them. I also wanted to inspire them to create a keepsake and tradition to be passed on to their children.

Well reader! I encourage you to do the same and write that letter. Even if you have a child already of a particular age, go back and write the letter of how you felt that day. Present the letter as a gift, and as a way to reach and connect with your daughter.

If you had a child that did not make it upon delivery, I encourage you to do the same as a way of healing and to share with their living siblings.

LETTER TO MY NEWBORN

July 11, 1988

Dear Baby Girl,

I must thank God for answering my prayers. He kept you safe in my womb and blessed me with a healthy baby girl. Excuse me baby while I give God the glory for blessing us with you. I prayed, "Thank you Lord! Without you, I know this would not have been possible. God, please know that I do not take on this task lightly. I know that you have kept your end of the bargain and I will do what your word instructs me to do. I will raise her in your word so that as she grows older, she will never depart."

Okay, back to the beautiful little baby in my arms, please know that I am so grateful that everything went well. It was a very long labor, but worth every minute. There is a saying anything worth having is worth waiting for, and that is so true. You have all ten fingers and ten toes, a beautiful little face and I think you are perfect. Looking into your eyes, I am a bit overwhelmed by the huge responsibility you are going to be. Will John, by the way, that is your dad, and I have what it takes to be the best mommy and daddy for you? Oh, my God, your innocence brings tears to my eyes. Your father and I cannot believe that together, we have created such a beautiful girl. Men are different from us ladies; they have a strong protective instinct. Therefore, when the nurse told us that you were a natural sucker, which was a compliment indicating you were smart from the start, your dad did not like the way that sounded. He growled at her and said, "That's not funny." She laughed and said, "You men are so silly."

We named you Jeanette Joyce in honor of both of your beautiful grandmothers. Your maternal grandmother Jeanette is in heaven, and I know she is an angel, assigned just for you. She will forever look after you. However, I sit here looking at you, filled with questions and doubts. Will I be a good mother to you? Do I have what it takes? Your grandmother died when I was so young, and I am so young, but I know as I sit here and look at you at this moment there is no way I can fail you.

Today, I promise to love you, as you matter a lot. I promise to listen as if everything you say is important. I am not perfect, so I know there will come a day when you may say, "Mom you suck at listening." I vow to give you the things you need to make you a strong woman who values herself and treats others with kindness. I need you to listen to me. I am going to give you the advice to protect yourself in certain situations, but I need you to follow it. I have so many experiences to share with you, and I hope you will take heed, so you will not have to experience everything to understand the consequences. If I tell you the stove is hot, you do not need to touch it to confirm, no, baby girl; you do not. There will be times when I will not do what you want me to. There will be times when we will not agree with each other, but know that I have good intentions.

Your father is my boo! God chose him for you and me. He is a man of character, honor and fiercely loyal.

Just a little advice even though I am sure you will not remember this. If a man loves his mother, he will love you more. Your father loves his, and that made me love him even the more. He is not a random person that I did not give thought or concern as to the role he would play in your life.

You have been born into a family that has great values and expectations. To be honest, I was a bit overwhelmed by the pride the Young's have and the traditions they hold sacred. You will come to know them for yourself, and you will realize that as one of them, you have a responsibility to uphold the Young name. You will be happy, kind, smart, God fearing and most of all you will be loved. I rebuke any spirit that is not of God. I speak well into your life.

If I am not living up to my end of the bargain as your mother, I give you permission to sit me down respectfully and let me know where I am falling short. I desire to be the best mom that I can be. I want us to understand each other with an open line of communication.

When God gave you to me, I promised God that I would give you back to Him. In a couple of months, we will get you a beautiful dress and have you dedicated, so I can give your spirit back to God and thank Him for blessing us with you. We will worship the Lord together, and you will wear the best dresses to church. I promise you will come to know God for yourself. As you go through life's many trials and tribulations, I want you to know God is there for you, and He will never leave nor forsake you.

I know I have laid a lot on you at only two hours old, but I have so many dreams for you that I can barely stand it. Remember this always; you're the daughter of the most High God. You are entitled to all He has set aside for you if you walk in His will. I love you, and God will always love you more.

Love you from the depths of my soul,
Mommy

February 15, 1991

Hello My Almost Valentine Baby,

I cannot believe God has blessed me with yet another beautiful baby girl. You are perfect and have the most beautiful face I have ever seen. I am honored to be your mom. Your dad has been bugging me asking if I will have you on Valentine's Day the day of love. I kept telling him how would I know but God will determine when you are born. You were five weeks early, and boy was I nervous when the contractions started. I was not sure it would be safe for you to come out. Nevertheless, here you are 6 lbs. 12 oz. and healthy. We named you Jahnique, which came from your dad's name, and mine combined, as you are the best of both of us. Your middle name is Joy and that you are. It is also your dad's favorite song.

    I am looking into your beautiful brown eyes, and I am wondering what you will be when you grow up and how you are going to be as a young woman. I know I am rushing your little life, but birth is the beginning of some many things. I am just excited about your future! Guess what you have a big sister who is going to love you, and cannot wait to meet you. Your dad is going to bring her later to see you.

    Your dad is so excited as you were the first that he actually got to see come into this world; he cut the cord and everything. The love in his eyes for you made me want to cry. The good thing for you is he is experienced now with taking care of a baby, so when he changes you, things might not be so rough (that's our little secret).

You are being born into a proud family the Young's have quite a bit of expectation and traditions, but I trust you will fit right in. There is a place carved out just for you. I cannot believe we have two daughters, I can't wait to dress you girls alike, and you are going to love it.

When God gave you to me, I promised God that I would give you back to Him. In a couple of months, we will get you a beautiful dress and have you dedicated, so I can give your spirit back to God and thank Him for blessing us with you. We will worship the Lord together, and you will wear the best dresses to church. I promise you will come to know God for yourself. As you go through life's many trials and tribulations, I want you to know God is there for you, and He will never leave nor forsake you.

I know I have laid a lot on you at only the first hours of your life, but I have so many dreams for you that I can barely stand it. Remember this always; you are the daughter of the most High God. You are entitled to all He has set aside for you if you walk in His will. I love you, and God will always love you more. I want you to know that you were born to two parents that truly love each other and wanted you. We are a family, and we promise to take care of you as best we know how. Welcome to our world baby girl.

Love you from the depths of my soul,
Mommy

May 5, 1997

Hello Baby Girl,

It is Cinco de Mayo, a day your Latin friends love to celebrate. On this day, as you get older you will learn all that goes on, and you may join the festivities. You were about three weeks early and born by a cesarean birth. I was so scared for both of us. The reason we had to have surgery to deliver you was because you refused to turn around. The doctors attempted to turn you around several times but to no avail. Therefore, when I went into labor, they had to get you out as safely as they could. Let me tell you baby girl you gave me the scare of my life when they first pulled you out of my belly because you did not make a sound. I was holding my breath waiting to hear the wail that I had heard two times before. I am laying here helpless, the doctors and nurses are all busy trying to get you breathing, and I am almost screaming why she is not crying. Let me tell you that, to me, those moments were forever but in reality within seconds no longer than a minute, I could hear you cry. Even though it was faint, you were crying. For the first two days of your life, you were in the neonatal nursery where they watched over you, and I prayed, your daddy prayed, your Grammy prayed and to God be the Glory you were fine.

You were named in honor of your aunt Lorri who preceded you in death, but she was such an awesome woman we wanted her legacy to live on. However, we are a family of J's so there is how the name Jorri came and your middle name is Jahnay like your daddy Johnny. He was a little perturbed by the change in spelling, but he will get over it. You are such a pleasant baby, so beautiful and brown; I cannot stop looking at you because once again I can't believe your mine God has given me another healthy baby girl. You are the first one that I allowed the doctors to tell me what I would be having because your two sisters were so excited to know if you were going to be a sister or a brother. I only wanted to have a healthy baby, so I was blessed either way.

I know I have said this before but what a blessing it is to go in the labor and delivery room again and come out with a healthy baby. I know it could have been much different so for that I am so grateful. I cannot wait to see all that you become and accomplish. Your dad is so excited as you were the first cesarean birth he witnessed them opening my stomach to take you out. He was super brave, as I would have been grossed out. He stood by our side the whole time. The love in his eyes for you made me want to cry. The good thing for you is he is experiencing taking care of a baby, so when he changes you, things might not be so rough (that's our little secret).

You are being born into a proud family the Young's have quite a bit of expectancy and traditions, but I trust you will fit right in. There is a place carved out just for you. I cannot believe we have three daughters and I can't wait to dress you girls alike. You are going to love it!

When God gave you to me, I promised God that I would give you back to Him. In a couple of months, we will get you a beautiful dress and have you dedicated, so I can give your spirit back to God and thank Him for blessing us with you. We will worship the Lord together, and you will wear the best dresses to church. I promise you will come to know God for yourself. As you go through life's many trials and tribulations, I want you to know God is there for you, and He will never leave nor forsake you.

    I know I have laid a lot on you at only the first hours of your life, but I have so many dreams for you that I can barely stand it. Remember this always; you are the daughter of the most High God. You are entitled to all He has set aside for you if you walk in His will. I love you, and God will always love you more. I want you to know that you were born to two parents that deeply love each other and wanted you. We are a family, and we promise to take care of you as best we know how. Welcome to our world baby girl.

Love you from the depths of my soul,
Mommy

It Worked for Me

January 1, 2002

Dear Baby Girl,

You were born on the first day of the year 2002 and the first baby born at Winthrop University Hospital. It is in the books baby girl! You are so pretty, you have chinky eyes, and your hair is bone straight. Many of the guests that have come to the hospital think you are an Asian baby. Well, the joke was on them when they saw your dad and me. I have to tell you that you were the hardest labor of them all. I went into premature labor on September 11 the day terrorist took four planes in three different locations and ran them into buildings. It was the worst terrorist attack on American soil. It was chaotic that day your dad was so worried about your uncle Larry who is a cop in New York City; you will meet him later. Thank God, he was ok, and you were not born that day however for the next three months I was in false labor every week until you finally made your entrance into this world. Your Aunt Ronnie nicknamed you 'terror in the womb' because you tried to make your appearance on the day of the 9/11 attacks. We used to giggle a lot about that. However, you are nothing like that but are my little blessing from God, and one day you will realize why it is great to be born on New Year's Day.

    We named you Jalena Joelle because I thought that name had so much personality and it matched you to the tee. Okay, your dad will say he came up with the name Jalena because I wanted to name you Jalen and he said that was a boy's name but the truth is Jalena sounds prettier, just like you.

I am so humbled as I lay here with you in my arms to once again go into the labor and delivery room for the fourth time and come out with a healthy baby girl. I did say girl again! I cannot lie to you I did hope to get a different result, but you are so beautiful I can only feel blessed. Your sisters are super excited to meet you. Guess what? Your oldest sister has bought the outfit you are going to come home in with her own money. You will come to understand how special that is as you get to know her. You are such a lucky little lady that has three big sisters that cannot wait to love and spoil you. Take advantage of all they have to offer you for they came ahead of you to help lead your way. Your dad is sitting in the room looking over at us with so much love in his eyes we are pretty lucky to have him.

Your dad is so excited as once again he got to see his last baby girl come into the world; he cut the cord and everything. The love in his eyes for you made me want to cry. The good thing for you is he is experienced now with taking care of a baby, so when he changes you, things might not be so rough (that's our little secret).

You are being born into a proud family the Young's have quite a bit of expectation and traditions, but I trust you will fit right in. There is a place carved out just for you. I cannot believe we have four daughters I can't wait to dress you girls alike, you are going to love it.

When God gave you to me, I promised God that I would give you back to Him. In a couple of months, we will get you a beautiful dress, and we will have you dedicated, so I can give your spirit back to God and thank Him for blessing us with you. We will worship the Lord together, and you will wear the best dresses to church. I promise you will come to know God for yourself. As you go through life's many trials and tribulations, I want you to know God is there for you, and He will never leave nor forsake you.

    I know I have laid a lot on you at only the first hours of your life, but I have so many dreams for you that I can barely stand it. Remember this always; you are the daughter of the most High God. You are entitled to all He has set aside for you if you walk in His will. I love you, and God will always love you more. I want you to know that you were born to two parents that madly love each other and wanted you we are a family and we promise to take care of you as best we know how. Welcome to our world baby girl.

Love you from the depths of my soul,
Mommy

I wrote those letters to each of my daughters so they would know what I was thinking the minute they were born. In reflection after each birth, I focused on the pain I endured and not on the blessing I received. However, I think once you put aside the pain you can embrace the moment and all the beauty that is within. Therefore, I charge you to write a letter to your newborn as well. Whether you choose to write it or record it express all of the love, hope, and dreams you have for them. The birth of a child is such a beautiful experience, and it should be captured. That special moment defines a lot in your life; so, take the time to preserve it. Even if your child is older, I encourage you to write the letter. Go back to that day and the moment you heard your baby cry or first held her.

    I hope that this will become a tradition that you will start for yourself and then pass it on to the generations to come so we have a living record of our children to share with their children and so on. I personally think it is beautiful and I wish I had a letter from my mom because who knew our time would be so short. I wish I had something from her to tell me what she wished and hoped for me.

It Worked For Me...

Many young girls and women question why their mom picked that particular man to be their father. This portion of the book is especially for those, my girls included, who have that question. The relationship between a father and daughter can be complex, but my views are from one who would have loved to have a father in her life. I have realized a few things from having a husband that is an awesome father.

1. Whether we understand it or not, parents are prepared and predestined by God.
2. Fathers do not think or love like mothers.
3. Consider this, trust your mom's judgment there was something about your father that she knew would be good for you.
4. If you had the chance to interview him, you probably would have picked him too.
5. Your dad is your first boyfriend so try to get that relationship right for it will affect so many of your future relationships.
6. Ask the woman who never had her dad in her life how she feels.

SORRY YOU COULD NOT INTERVIEW YOUR FATHER

Girls, I can remember the joy your father had in his eyes when he laid his eyes on you the day you were born. His eyes became glued to you, and he promised from that day he would take care of you, protect you with all of him, and let no danger come your way. I am writing this with a partial understanding of what a man feels towards his daughter and the expectations he has for her.

A fathers' love is so different from yours, or your mother's, within his mind. If he provides for you, protects you, shelters you from hurt and respect you, that means he loves you. I listen to so many women with daddy issues, and I say I wish for just one moment I could relate.

My dad was non-existent in my life. He dropped in and out, but when I think about it, he gave me the best he could. I can remember thinking that he loved my brother more, he was spending all this time with him, and that he did not love me. Then I found out from my brother he did not give him much more than he gave me. When I was a child, I thought as a child, and when I became a woman, I thought like a woman. I forgave him for all he did not do and was grateful for the things he did.

I have two candid memories of my dad one is when I was about six years old. It was Thanksgiving night, and he came to take me to my grandma's house for

It Worked for Me

dinner. We were walking to her house we stopped at the corner of my block. He then lifts me up and starts to throw me up in the air, and I said, "Daddy stop you're scaring me." His response was, "I am going to throw you up to the light." Now picture the light post in Brooklyn if your familiar or any tall silver light post in your town over 30 feet high. Then God sends my cousin Phillip, who will forever be my hero, around the corner, and he made my dad stop and took me home. I was so grateful that he showed up and I never forgot that.

The second memory is the year before my Dad died he came to visit and took me to dinner! We ate, talked, laughed and it was so nice to be with him. After talking for a while, he shared the Veterans Administration made a mistake and told him he had HIV. I looked at him and told him to take care of himself. I can remember his eyes being so clear and his voice super crisp. I fell in love with my dad that day the way a girl should love her father. It was the one and only honest conversation we ever had. He told me he loved me, was proud of the young woman I was becoming and that he was glad we had that time to talk. I did not know that would be our last real conversation, as that next summer he died I was only 20 years old, and I was motherless and fatherless.

When I first met your father, he was so sweet, and I thought this guy is too good to be true. However, what you saw is what you got. I witnessed his strong family ties, he loved his mom, sister, and aunts and he loved God, what man could be a better father. Well over the years, I found out that you girls did not see him the same way. I realize that maybe you should have interviewed him for yourself, but then I think God did that when he paired your dad and me together and blessed us with you.

Again, men and women equate love differently. He always took care of your physical needs while you screamed what about your emotions. There is a popular saying with states, "men are from Mars and women are from Venus." I believe this statement to be true. My babies, you will never know how many nights I cried for you, thinking that I had failed you by not standing up for you. Then I say how would you find your voice if I kept intervening.

So many times, I felt like a referee in the middle of the battles between your father and you. I rang that bell so many times having to cool everyone down. I realized one day that I was not helping and that you all needed to work it out on your own. I needed to stay out the middle because it was killing me and dividing you all. Guess what? One day I turned around, and you were co-conspirators against me. There were times that I did not like the way things went down, but I realized it was not my battle. I had to go to the Lord in prayer, lay the situations down before the throne and ask God to fix it. For the most part, He did.

I can remember as little girls each one of you would run to the door like the King had come to our doorstep. When your daddy came home, he was all you wanted. He ate that up, he loved you more, worked harder, sacrificed and did all he could to make your dreams come true. I know sometimes you have been disappointed in his reaction to your accomplishment, your pain, your story and your drama, but know that he loves you through all of it but he is not a girl that would show emotion.

Jeanette, I remember when you were about five years old and got your little bike with the training wheels. Dad decided to teach you how to ride without the training wheels, you went to the park, and you pedaled, and he chased you. When he let go you fell, he helped you up kissed your booboo. Then you took him by the hand, and you told him, "Sit down, Daddy, I know what the problem is." You looked him in his eye, and you said, "I have to get my confidence. I know that you will be right here to catch me if I fall." That day you learned how to ride a two-wheeler and when your Dad brought you home, you were so excited to tell me about your adventure. Little did you know your dad had tears in his eyes because he realized his little girl was growing up and understanding some of the lessons he had taught you. From you he learned how to teach your sisters to ride their bikes, they learned younger and they were so confident because he stood behind them and waited for them to ask him to let go. Jeanette, you may say that your father has never accepted you for who you are, but I will say that he has done the best he could based on what he believes. Know that he has always loved you, tried to protect you and would not disown you. Trust me; Daddy has your back.

Jahnique, I know that you believe that your father did not respect your privacy or feelings. However, you have admitted knowing that your dad loves you and always looked out for you.

Jorri, you have been a hard read, but I think you think Dad does not trust you to make your own decisions. However, you must also bow to the same tune of daddy loving you. His protection is always present because he will pick you up from work, worry about how you are getting home when hanging out with friends and will sit up waiting until you get home.

Jalena, you have touched the soft and generous side of your father. If you get him to go to the mall and get you new sneakers the day they come out and without it being your birthday, wow. Your sisters would agree that he is a lot more patient with you. And, in your eyes daddy is perfect.

I am sorry that you could not interview your father, but I still believe until this day that I made a great choice when I picked him. You could not have asked for a more caring, patient and loyal father. I beg for you to understand that dad may not always say or do the right thing, but you best believe the next person better not hurt or disappoint you, including me. I know that he means well, even if his words are not flowery his deeds are consistent, and he always had your best interest at heart.

I believe that fathers and daughters will always share a special bond as do mothers and daughters. Your dad is your first guy, and he shows you what to expect from a man, so I hope I choose well. I don't think we are ever able to realize how unique our dads are until we mature in our thinking. Dads look out for you even when you do not want them to; they don't know how not to. So when you are shaking your head saying really, just remember that is what he knows how to do which is love, protect and provide for his little girl.

Each of us has taught our dad a little bit about being a dad; I am sure we all would describe our dad a little different. Your father will grow and he will change and mature in some ways and others, not at all.

Daughters, do you realize that some of your fathers were dads for the first time with you and that some of them did not have a dad where they could imitate or learn? That means, most of the time he was winging it as he went along. I am not saying he was always right, but he kept trying.

Specifically for Dads

Dads, if I could give you a little advice, I would say...

1. Listen to your daughters, get to know her, be a friend and love her through the physical and emotional pain.
2. PMS is real and should be respected and understood. As I write this, I am laughing out loud because my husband always says it's not real you and don't have to act like that.
3. Be careful in how you handle her mother in front of her because she is going to be scarred by your actions. I have a friend who is aware of her dad's infidelity, and it has caused her a great deal of pain as well as trust issues. Her dad is aware that she knows and his lack of action has caused much division and discord.
4. Be willing to apologize when you are wrong. A simple, I am so sorry baby girl for disappointing you, goes a long way.
5. Your daughter expects you to listen and communicate with her. Your daughter needs your approval and your opinion matters. However, she also expects you to have her back. You may not agree at times but stop, think and try to see a situation from her side. A girl feels like she can take on the world when her daddy has her back.
6. Most importantly, I want to remind you that you are your daughter's first boyfriend. She will look for the example you set in every man she meets, so take it seriously.

Your daughter needs your love, attention, encouragement and you to tell her how beautiful she is. Make sure she knows your love as she will meet a man and he may try to tear her down. However, she won't let him because she will hear her daddy saying you are beautiful and you can have and be anything you want because you believe in her.

Part Two
For Us Who Have Girls

THE EARLY YEARS

As I write about the first few years of motherhood and the changes, my girls and I went through. I often asked these questions:

1. Where is the parent manual?
2. Who is going to help me when I don't know what to do?

The first year or so was relatively easy, no issues, when they cry you know they need feeding, changing or holding and that usually solved the problem. However, then the questions and situations arise that we are not prepared for, and there is no manual or instructions on how to answer. Therefore, I realized early on that 90% of parenting is instinct. There is no rulebook, don't be too hard on yourself and you will learn as you go along. By the fourth child, you will be writing books.

So, that baby that was just in your arms so helpless and depending on you for everything is now becoming a person exploring, inquiring and trying to figure out all the things around them. They have begun to develop a personality, and you can see some of yourself in them, and you are wondering why God won't let time stand still so you can capture all the moments in their lives. I am sure many mothers and fathers have moments in the journey of parenting that stick out in their mind. Some things will bring a smile, while others will make you cry. So here, I will share a few memories that will make you laugh, and some make you cry, but the main thing to remember is life is all about the moments.

There was a moment between my daughter and her father that I will never forget; it was so tender that it makes me smile. He was on his way to work one morning when our daughter Jeanette was about two years old at the time. She was sitting on the couch talking to her daddy, and she told him that her baby doll needed shoes. I looked at him, and he had tears in his eyes because he was working so hard to keep shoes on her little feet. She was just so carefree, and we were so proud that she had already started to take responsibility for her baby.

The next memory I will share may require tissue or a glass of wine to keep your nerves together. I share with you the worst day of my 25 years on this planet earth and one of the biggest tests of my faith and one of the grandest testaments to God's mercy and grace, so here we go.

In one moment, she was sitting on the floor as I was exercising on my stationary bike. She was throwing some cards in the air, I told her several times to stop, and in a blink of an eye, she stumbled, and her hand got stuck in the chain of that bike. I thought I would die from her screams and my heart was breaking one piece at a time. I had to pull her hand out of the chain. God's grace got me through that moment. As I write this, I am crying remembering how horrible I felt.

We get an ambulance, and they take us to Booth Memorial Hospital in Queens, New York and that is when God's hand started to move. We are now in the emergency room, the look on the doctor's faces do not

It Worked for Me

offer any hope, and they are talking about amputating my baby's fingers. However, before they make any decision, they have to call a pediatric surgeon. God sent in a surgeon who happened to work at Bellevue Hospital where world-renowned hand specialists also worked. He said let me give a call to my two buddies that specialize in microsurgery which is what my baby would need to save any or either of her fingers. I left out one detail; it was her left hand the pointer and the tall man or center finger. He comes back and instructs the doctors to prepare her hand so they can move her to another hospital; the doctors are willing to try to save her fingers. We got back in an ambulance on our way to New York City and arrived at Bellevue Hospital. The two doctors (hand surgery specialists) explained what the surgery would entail and the expected duration of time, it would take. It was the longest five and half hours of my life, but they came out and told us they were able to reconnect the blood vessels but only time would tell if they would work. I thanked them, but so riddled with guilt; I could not hear or see God.

The next days were so crazy; they had to use leeches to try and rejuvenate the blood. Can you imagine seeing leeches biting on her little hand? It was horrible, but a necessity. In the end, she did lose one digit on the pointer finger on her wedding hand. Oh my God! What have I done, she is going to hate me. The guilt was so heavy at a point I was ashamed of what happened and thought my husband blamed me. I did not know how to deal with all of it. Of course, he did not blame me, I blamed myself but that is what the devil does, he whispers in your ear when you are down. I was devastated and could barely look at her hand, God had trusted me with this perfect baby, and she was hurt on my watch. Now healing was in order; I had to forgive myself and realize an accident is just what it means – an unfortunate incident that happens unexpectedly and unintentionally resulting in damage or injury. It was not a punishment or a reflection of my parenting, it just happened. I forgave myself, my marriage was stronger, and my prayer life was renewed.

I know most people are like my husband and I, in that, we live to create a home and environment for our children, where they will prosper and grow into young people free to thrive. It's a parent's sacrifice to secure a home in which their family will grow and share many moments. I can remember when we went to buy our first home, we only had the two older girls at that time, but we knew our family would continue to grow. We looked for a house that would become a home for us.

When I think about the first time we came to see what would become our home the thing that stuck out the most for me was my little girls running on the porch, the sound of their feet and the laughter as they chased each other. They looked at us and said we are going to live in this mansion (It was a 4-bedroom Victorian, but out of the mouths of babes). We looked at each other and knew right then that it would be our home. We moved in, and our neighbors' children were now becoming the girls' new friends. Therefore, here comes a new life lesson for them, they had to understand the concept of having a friend; they must be friends with them. They had to learn some hard lessons about people, what they would and would not do.

It Worked for Me

When the girls were little my oldest daughter Jeanette would give away all her snacks and then cried when she didn't have any. When she went to their (friends) houses, they never gave her any snacks, or they would go in the house and eat their snack without offering her any. I told her so many times not to give away all of your things or you will be left with nothing. Also, other people will not return the favor so save a little for you.

Now for the excitement! They were going to school, and I had to pray because all of my home training is sufficient for them to behave properly. I remember getting a call from the school that there was an incident; I was like "Lord! What could have happened to my child?" I got there, and they told me that a teacher had taken off his shirt in the classroom and my daughter Jahnique went to report to the principal. I was very curious, and I needed to know more. They said that she asked for permission to go to the bathroom, but she went and told the principal that the teacher was in the classroom taking off his shirt and that was inappropriate. The principal sent her back to the class, when she got back the teacher asked, "Why were you gone so long?" and she told him she went to report to the principal what he did in front of the girls. Upon questioning the teacher, he denied, but the principal noticed he did not have on the same shirt he was wearing earlier. The principal removed the teacher from the class.

I shared this as someone may not always take the side of their child, but I want you to remember that your child deserves the benefit of the doubt, they're not always telling stories. Encourage them to be brave enough to tell on someone and not be intimidated.

I can remember whenever I went to a parent-teacher conference for Jeanette, the teachers always said: "I wish I had 30 of your daughter". However, when I went to the same set of teachers a year or two later for Jahnique, they would ask if she was also my daughter because she is the exact opposite of her sister. I would just smile, as Jeanette had always been a people pleaser, Jahnique not so much.

I can remember when Jeanette was nominated to the Mayor's cabinet program at her school. It required you to go to the Mayor's office and spend the day, receive a citation and have your picture hung up at the High School. It was quite a big deal. When Miss Jahnique got to the fourth grade, and she wasn't nominated, she couldn't believe it. She came home and said, "Mommy, I thought if my sister won so would I." That was her first lesson on entitlement and knowing that in some circumstances you won't be able to ride the coattails of others. She did realize that from that day, she had to put in the work for what she wanted.

I don't know about you, but the one thing I dreaded the most was the question of spending the night at a friend's house, especially, when they were in adolescence. I could always hear my mother in law telling me that your babies are not library books, do not lend them out, they may not return the same way. Jahnique would always ask if she could spend the night at her friend's house. I was always so afraid there would be someone in their households that wasn't right. She always looked at me with unshed tears wanting to go to this friend or that friend's house. I always had to investigate the scene beforehand; sometimes she could go, other times not. Nevertheless, I will say that we should always arm our children with examples and strategies/solutions in the event one of certain scenarios arising. For example, I told her that when her friend's crazy Uncle Mike comes out of the attic or basement, and she did not feel comfortable, she could always use me as her excuse to leave. I gave her so many outs for the awkward moments.

- I didn't do the dishes I got to go home
- My mom is bipolar she forgot she said I couldn't stay
- I got smart with my mom, and she said either I come home now or she is coming here to whoop me

It's not about us parents not wanting our children to go to their friends' houses; we just want to protect them from incidents that will not be forgotten and sometimes have irreversible effects. I do know that there are lessons to be learned when you fellowship with other families, memories that last a lifetime and that create lifelong relationships. They also learned to be grateful for the things provided in their homes and realized what they took for granted is another person's luxury.

So many memories come to mind, even though I have only shared a few. Perhaps you have a few memories of your own with becoming a parent and all that it entails. Keep those memories in your arsenal so that you can create your own box of "It Worked For Me" Tips to help another parent.

It Worked for Me...

When I think about raising my girls, I always thought about them as individuals and tried to meet them at their needs. Here are a few things to help you remember and a brief list of what I learned. We must work to relate to our millennials because we know they seem like aliens sometimes.

1. No two children are like they are all different and must be handled differently.
2. Teenagers are people too, they must be heard, and you will learn a lot.
3. To remember I was a teenager once and know what I was thinking and feeling. It is important to keep that in mind when dealing with our girls.
4. Not to take their immaturity personal they haven't been here as long as I have.
5. Remind them that every action has a consequence good or bad!
6. Always encourage them never be ashamed of being smart!
7. Teach your children early on not be a follower but to lead the pack!
8. You are not your child's friend! You can be friendly though it will pay off it's like any relationship it deserves nurturing.
9. Do not be afraid to say No! Life is full of No's, and it's best for them to hear it from someone who loves them.
10. Children are like cakes with all different ingredients, bake at different temperatures and take time to rise.

11. A little fear is healthy, but respect is golden!
12. Tell your children early on they must set goals. Doing so will allow them to have a plan, and very little time to deviate. Always have a plan for it will keep you out of trouble.
13. Learning from my mistakes is necessary. However, paying attention to the mistakes of others makes the journey a lot less bumpy.

A Teenager, Who Are You?

Let's get right to it and talk about the teenager. I don't know about you but did your kids lose their mind when they turned 13! My question is what do children think happens when you turn "13"? Did someone tell them that when they become teenagers, they no longer have to listen and can do whatever they like? However, we know that this is when the whole game changes. The decisions they make at this time can change their life so we must pay closer attention to what they are doing. So how do we deal with a millennial at this stage?

- ✓ Confront them immediately when the battle (boundary) lines become crossed
- ✓ Cancel the "yes" fest! Although you don't want to say no, you will have to say it more in their teenage years
- ✓ Do not be swayed by their emotions! Through the tears and mumbling, they will be fine
- ✓ Teach them that it's never too early to set goals
- ✓ Encourage them to make good and be proud of themselves

Don't be afraid; they will grow up and realize that you were only doing what is best for them. However, parents, we will fight and win. Children, we love you, all that we do is for your wellbeing.

The analogy I would like to use for the teenage years is the baker and his many recipes for all the different

It Worked for Me

cakes he prepares. I like to think that our children are different types of cakes, for instance, what you use to make a German chocolate cake will not work when making a pineapple upside down cake. When you are raising your daughters, you must realize each cake will require different ingredients as well as take a little longer or shorter to bake.

Let me briefly share this with you that two of my four cakes have baked, are out of the oven, and I would like to think they came out pretty damn good. Currently, the third one is rising nice and looks good. She had to bake at a lower temperature. The last one pretty much just went in the oven with ingredients that were complicated and tedious, but it looks like it's going to rise. I will have to let you know later on how those cakes turned out.

My first-born is Jeanette is a like a German chocolate cake it takes a lot of ingredients and patience for it to rise as well as taste good. She was my first from scratch cake where I had to learn how to sift flour, in other words, be patient and work all the lumps out. Then I had to learn how to mix the ingredients one at a time start with the foundations of love, patience, kindness, and discipline and when the batter was all together and ready I then had to know when to apply them so this cake would be good. Then there is the frosting called self-esteem and character you have to help them apply just right because the presentation is everything. I want to share a bit about her and her role in our family being the firstborn. I have to say she took being the big sister seriously and did her best to be a good example. I can remember her going through such an identity crisis and me not being able to figure out how to reach her. I started putting little notes in her bag telling her that she was beautiful, kind, special and designed for greatness. I must say she didn't change abruptly at 13; she subtly started changing in high school; she prided herself in her schoolwork so when that started to slip, I knew she was trying her hand at being a teenager. She started cutting class and wouldn't come straight home as instructed, she was screaming, "Whoop me," and we did. I cannot forget when she went to the store with her dad and sister, and she stole some film.

The security guard grabbed the back of her jacket, her dad walked up and said, "Excuse me! You better take your hands off her." The security guard said she had something in her pocket that belonged to them. My husband was so embarrassed when he pulled that film out of her pocket, and she acted so toughly that day it broke my heart. She was screaming for attention, and I tried so hard to avoid that moment. Her dad gave her first real beating, and I think I cried more than she did. However, I knew we had to stop her before we lost her. I admit I admired her loyalty to her family as when she went to school with lumps, bumps, and she never uttered a word. She understood her punishment was warranted and that it was for her own good. She also knew that the consequences were greater than the story. I always told her we loved her and would never do anything to hurt her. Even though people of authority told her that if we hit her, it was abuse, she understood it was love. If we didn't care, we would have let her keep doing what she was doing and let her bump her head so many more times. I must tell you that we were able to work through those times and she graduated from High School with an Advanced Regents Diploma. My girl went on to graduate from college not bad for my first from scratch cake!

> **Millennial Parenting Tip!**
> A refusal to correct is just like
> a refusal to love your child.

My second born is Jahnique who is a good old fashion pineapple upside down cake, because, she did everything in reverse. When making this cake you put the top on the bottom, and then you flip to see the beautiful cake it is. I must say that she helped me to grow up and become a more assertive parent because she challenged me every step of the way. I can say she has raised me well! When I said right, she said wrong! If I said the sky is blue, she said not exactly it looks a little gray! This young lady is the Queen of BUT I would say to her "ok," I heard your opinion, and I gave mine. Too bad for her my word was final after several heated debates. I was so surprised that she still had teeth for all the pops she got in the mouth; I must admit this may not have worked on her because she never stopped talking. What did work was me instructing her on how to and when to speak. How she can be heard without being rude. I like to say that made her more assertive and determined to get her point across. She always was an honest child; I asked and always waited with baited breath for her answer because God only knew what she was going to say.

She taught me to listen and to have patience because she had to express herself. I had to learn that our millennial children deserve to be heard. I had to teach her how to end a discussion with an understanding that not everything will turn out in her favor in every situation. Take it as a lesson learned, and it's okay to disagree. She also taught me about group dating by coming and asking could she go to the movies with friends. After hearing the list of friends, I realized this chick was trying to pull a fast one by trying to set up a group date way before the set age requirement to do so. She was creative I have to give her that. This one went on to graduate High School in three years with a Regent's Diploma, and she went away to college and graduated in four years. Not too bad for the second cake, I am on my way to becoming a professional baker.

> **Millennial Parenting Tip!**
> Be willing to listen, you might learn something.

My third daughter Jorri is such a blessing. She is amazing and has not changed one bit thank you, Jesus! She is an old-fashioned pound cake. She had simple ingredients but had to be watched as she baked so she would rise just right. This young lady makes me proud because she was so simple to raise and the only requirements were love and patience. She is the same sweet girl that she started as and she has not given us one day of heartache. She is an even-tempered young lady. Let us not get it twisted she has had her moments with being stubborn, but so that is where the patience

It Worked for Me

came in. I had to learn to wait her out. One of her main challenges was her height she was 5' 10" in the fifth grade. You can imagine the mixed emotions being tall brought on, but I always told her to keep her head up and work her height. Never allow anyone to make her feel she is too anything. Moreover, she is just right! As time went on, she realized boys are immature at any height. I encouraged her to join clubs, sports, and events that would highlight her height and increase her confidence. Today she walks the runaway every time she walks out the door. The other thing I contribute to her success is having a great group of friends in which they've had an ongoing competition for who would get the best grades who could complain about that. Jorri has also graduated from High School with her Advanced Regents Diploma and is currently entering her junior year in college. I guess I am getting the hang of this baking thing and perfecting these ingredients because these cakes are surely coming out good.

> **Millennial Parenting Tip!**
> Teach them to love what others consider awkward.

My baby girl Jalena is something else, a straight trip and just 15. She is the red velvet cake. The recipe is simple yet precise, and the frosting is everything. I would like to think that as you know better, you do better. By child number four and our maturity, things should be simpler. She is smart as a whip and started walking at eight months. She knew directions up and down as well as under and over and the distinction between hot and cold by one year old. I think, as older parents, we are just more relaxed, but this little child is running the joint. She has her father going to the mall to get a pair of sneakers for her on the day they come out. I did not recognize the man who asked me should he go to the mall before work because his daughter wanted the sneakers. It was not her birthday or anything! Floored, I said to myself, who is this man. Reader, I need you to understand that my husband is a no-nonsense kind of guy and he does not endorse any products or care about the latest trends. When he was willing to go out and get them for her with no occasion, that was a big deal. I think he realized that like all things we might have to change. What worked with one might not with the other. She is very fashion conscious and is a bit of trendsetter, so we encourage her to try her hand at entrepreneurship. So far, she has a personalized hoodie and t-shirt business. She is going into her sophomore year in high school, takes advanced classes and has a 90 average. We have no complaints. I can say she has not given me a day of trouble thank you, Jesus. I guess the moral of the story is when you perfect the ingredients the cake is sure to rise each time.

> **Millennial Parenting Tip!**
> Teach your child to capitalize financially
> on their interests.

Allow me to share a little about my childhood to get a better understanding of me as the author and the dynamics of my family. I am the youngest of six children, four older sisters, and one brother. My mother was a single mom, and she did her best to raise us into happy, healthy, and employed citizens. She did not slack on the discipline. Have you ever heard of someone getting in trouble for leaving the block? Well, I have, it was crazy. I was fifteen, I went to a friend's house, and she tore my butt up, hit me in the head with a crochet covered wooden heel shoe. My head was bust open, and I probably needed a stitch or two. You know what my mom said. I should not have made her do it – this lady is a cookoo. My sisters were always in trouble. My mom should have faced arrest for the whipping's we got. I remember one time where I received mercy when she came to a block party. I was doing my dance, and my friends were pointing behind me. I wasn't paying them any attention; I thought they were pointing to tell me a young man was behind me. Boy was I wrong! Little did I know my momma was behind me with her housedress on, no bra, (you can laugh now) you get the picture. However, she didn't beat me at the block party but rung my ear and told me to get my butt home. Her doing that was much better than a whipping at the party. Thank you, mom, for saving my social future!

I remember when I told my girls that I had a wig and a housecoat reserved for wear if they ever called me from their school saying they were was acting a fool. To date, I am proud to say the housecoat and wig have not visited the school. I always told them from little girls if you embarrass me, I would return the favor. Mothers don't be afraid to give these children a little fear of what you might do, believe me, they will be scared you just might do it and not try you. I would never want to go to the school looking like that, but they should be equally scared to embarrass me as if I did not give them any home training.

As this chapter ends, here are a few more tips that worked for me!

1. Teach your daughter to explore and try new things; do not let others opinions keep them in a social box.
2. Tell them, although their hormones will begin to rage, keep closed legs and an open mind.
3. Repeatedly speak over them and say that greatness is available to us all.

I have shared a lot but being a teenager is a lot! Remember being a teenager is a part of the journey so let's have a smooth ride, be smart, lead our daughters and don't follow their lead. If they make mistakes let it be because they wanted to do something not from following someone else.

It Worked For Me...

Being a listener will make you a good parent. You will hear things you don't want to, but you and your child will be better for it. Communication is a need in all relationships. As a parent, we must be reminded:

1. Confession is good for the soul.
2. Communication is key in every relationship even the one with our child.
3. We cannot only hear and deal with the things we like because we are raising whole children.
4. Being a parent your child can trust is important in their development of outside the home relationships.
5. Not to take ourselves so seriously.

60 Seconds of Confession

Many of us come from a time where we kept secrets or did not feel comfortable enough to share certain things with our parents. Let's face it! Nobody discussed things with our parents, so they didn't discuss it with us. However, we live in a society where everything is visual, and there is no possible way to avoid our children seeing things even with parental controls, etc. Additionally, we have so much in society that influences their opinions and even tries to answer their questions without having a direct conversation. That is why I used this strategy on my daughters called 60 Seconds of Confession.

During this time, they can tell me their inner thoughts or secrets with no consequence (at least at the time). I saw this as confession without the priest and a cleansing that allowed them the opportunity to share any hurt. It is also a way for me to offer guidance instead of them seeking it elsewhere and receiving bad information. I found out several things I didn't want to know and sometimes I had to stop the clock because it was way too much information. However, through it all, I learned so much about what was going on in my daughter's lives that I was clueless about. I prided myself on being in touch with my girls' sheesh was I wrong!

I started this when my oldest daughter Jeanette was a little girl one day she came in from school looking upset. I asked what was wrong. She said nothing, so I asked again, and she said nothing, again. I thought to myself something happened, how can I get her to confess. I told her I was going into my room to pray and God would tell me what happened. She said okay. I went into my room, got down on one knee, and she busted in the door and said no mom don't ask God I will tell you. It was such a simple thing that happened that day, but it gave me an idea of how to let her tell me what is going on. You know, how Catholics confess but without all of the formality. That was when my 60 seconds of confession was born. I needed to know about the things they were too scared to tell me so I could help them work through it.

Millennial Parenting Tip!
Find creative ways to snoop into their lives.

It will be hard, but we as parents must grow up a little. Understanding that our girls will not always do things, we approve of or expect. However, wouldn't you rather help them clean up or fix what they can with you than seek counsel from some other mixed up teenager? Worse, mix with some young man who has all his best interests at heart and not hers. I know I did.

My Jeanette has told me many things in our sessions that sometimes I wanted to tap out. I learned that it was an opportunity for me to learn from her and assess what her needs were. I had the invitation to intervene as well as guide her through some of life's situations. I remember the time she told me that she kissed a girl I was like what in my head, but I realized this was an opportunity to guide her. My first thought question was what does she mean she kissed a girl? Then I realized I could not create an awkward moment. She needed to understand that it did not define her or her position on her sexuality. Then she told me she had sex (holding my breath) but wait, with a boy! I thought something was brewing with the boy she spoke about, but I didn't think it was that deep. She was out of high school at this point. I didn't want to appear too excited, so I downplayed it. Inside I was jumping for joy (Prayers answered!). I calmed down a few weeks later she came to me and said it just did not do it for her. Then she told me so many things about her lifestyle and the things she was going through that I sometimes was clueless on how to help her, but I knew basic human relations, and I tried to guide her as best I could. Remember parents you won't know everything but be open to anything!

My daughter Jahnique never fell for the technique I must admit. When I gave her confession time, she would tell me she stole a pen or one time she said she kissed a boy and sure did like it. I asked how much and she said, "Not enough to forget that affection and foreplay are different." She was always quite the funny one.

The two baby girls, I used a different approach. I opened up our communication with laughter and acceptance, so they pretty much tell me all that is going on without a formal platform. I learned with the first two not to take myself so seriously and to let them live. They understood the rules of the house and respected them, and I must say I do not have many problems. I thank God that they want to talk to me, I do not have to force conversation when I sit and check in with them. I monitor their social media lives, but I express the values that we have and expect them to respect them. We have such an open relationship that I often have to check them on the parameters of our conversations, as sometimes they get a little loose with language and information.

> **Millennial Parenting Tip!**
> Establish a family code of honor and expectation of how they should respect themselves and their family name on social media and social settings.

I wanted to share this technique because I think mothers forget that their daughters need a platform to share without our mother hat on all the time. A minute of freedom to talk can lead to some pivotal moments. If you listen you will see who they are becoming, can help them to make some changes or encourage the path they are on.

    I listen to so many women with daughters, and the struggle to be in control is so volatile. Mom's you were young once remember that and know you are far smarter than her. Be a grown up and use your skills to affect positive change. We do not have to stand on our authority and bully our daughters. Remember, you are what you see. Use strategies that allow you both to get what you want. I am not saying in all things this will be effective, but in many instances, if you think about it and not react the minute she says the word boy or date, you may come to a resolution that will leave you in total control. I have learned these young people can be stubborn and will do wrong to make you angrier. The truth is no one wins.

Effective communication is necessary in any relationship! The relationship with our children is vital to every relationship they will have in their life.

> **Millennial Parenting Tip!**
> Don't be the first bully your child meets!

Show them kindness and compassion, and they will show it too. Children imitate the treatment received until someone shows them different. Do you want the influence of a random person to be the game changer for your daughter? I want you to embrace opportunities to talk and let them have a voice. Remember you are not raising your child for you, but for the world. They need to be able to survive.

It Worked for Me...

I am a parent that has many hopes and dreams for my girls and me. I encourage them daily to seek what will make them happy and do it every day. For me, I am on the brink of 50, and I am just starting to pursue my dreams. It's not too late for me but right in God's timing! Parent, I say to you it is never too late to pursue your dreams. If you dropped it, go back, pick it up and run with it. While doing that, here are a few more things you can say and do with your girl.

1. Tell her, a dream is a preview of your future if you pursue it.
2. Encourage her not to let anyone talk her out of your dream.
3. Remind her not to let anyone take her off her 'dream' course.
4. When discussing your child's dream with them, always give direction and encouragement. Remember they don't always know what to do to achieve it.
5. Teach her that financial success shouldn't measure a dream. If what she does brings her joy, she will be rich!

Dream Big Fear Little

"Be anxious for nothing, but in everything by prayer and supplication, with thanksgiving, let your requests be made known to God; and the peace of God, which surpasses all understanding, will guard your hearts and minds through Jesus Christ."
                                   –Philippians 4:6-7

I shared that scripture because it relaxes me when I am anxious and afraid. It also encourages me when I let the world steal my joy and make me think I can't. Parent, I want you to dream so big that nothing can hold or contain it. I want you to plan for it and never be discouraged. Make your request before God the minute you know that thing you were born to do. If it is his will, it will happen. Pray about it, be bold in your requests. God loves to hear our thoughts, as he already knows His plans for us. As you go through this journey, keep a journal and write down what you have accomplished and what the next steps are toward your goal. Doing this allows us to see the favor of God in our lives. Moreover, it is a reminder of how He has already blessed us. I remember hearing that if you do something you love you will feel like you never worked a day in your life. I want that for you so much that it's like an ache in my gut. Think about it, if your passion is public speaking, every time you have an engagement will be like the first time butterflies in your tummy, new expectations and your dream lived out once again. I don't know about you, but I would choose that.

It Worked for Me

What is a dream by Webster's definition? If defined as a noun, a series of thoughts, images, and sensations occurring in a person's mind during sleep. If defined as a verb, contemplating the possibility of doing something, or that something might be the case

Now that I have shared some encouraging words with you as a parent, please know, it's never too late to pursue a dream. I want you to take those same words I spoke to you and use them for your daughter. As I write this book, I am entering my 50th year of life. Did I have dreams when I was younger? Of course! However, I made the mistake of allowing people to discourage me. Sound familiar?

One thing I can say about millennials, they are go-getters and passionate about what they want to do once their mind is made up. It is never too late to be inspired by them, as I am daily. I wanted to do a comedic set; I can now cross that off my list. I wanted to become an author; you are reading the fulfillment of my dream.

Sometimes we give up because the dream seems too far-fetched or unattainable, but that is the devil trying to steal your joy. Remember his job is to steal, kill, and destroy. I want you and your daughter to fight and win. I know this book is about raising our daughter but part of raising them is leading by example on pursuing your dreams.

I remember getting a text from my daughter Jalena saying, "I want to be an oncology doctor because I want to encourage little girls and ladies that have lost their hair due to cancer. I want them to know that they're beautiful, their lives have meaning and not to give up."

I thought to myself how beautiful if she fulfills her dream she would not work one day in her life. I gave her practical thoughts and shared with her to understand she will experience death firsthand and will not be able to save everyone. Also, she would have to articulate to someone's loved one that they have passed away. I said, "I told you this because I want you to be prayerful that God prepares your heart for this assignment." I have been encouraging her to stay focused, study hard and hard and remember it is hard work to become a doctor. However, the reward will be great.

> **Millennial Parenting Tip!**
> Support your daughter with constant encouragement in what they would like to do and not what you want them to do!

My daughter Jeanette is the manager of a group home for adults with disabilities. However, her original dream was to be a physical therapist. What happened? Well, she got a job at a group home and found love and acceptance that I don't think she planned for or wanted initially. She has always been a renegade not conforming to the social expectations of others, and God has afforded her an environment that would be accepting. She started college away from home and failed miserably. I admit a portion of the blame was ours for not seeing she just was not ready. However, the other 95% came from her simply not saying she wasn't happy and did not want to stay. It was a lesson learned for us all and showed me that I needed to be less vested and let her be more invested and remember the statement it's not how we start but how we finished. She went to Nassau Community College for two years, finished at SUNY Oswego on the dean's list for a semester or two, and graduated with a Bachelor's in Health and Wellness. She has compassion for those who need a voice. I pray she will continue her education and pursue becoming a philanthropist to encourage others to help those who cannot help themselves. Ultimately I want her dreams to be fulfilled not my thoughts or ideas, all her.

My third daughter Jorri, I am watching her right now fresh out of high school just starting her higher education experience. She has a game plan, however, no passion. She desires to become a nurse. However, she is not committed. I told her to take her electives see what interest her. Then discuss with her counselor at the school what job would link with that interest. She has such personality and the warmest smile I have ever seen that beams from the inside out, and I know whatever she decides to do the people who work around her will be blessed as she brings the sunshine in the door with her.

> **Millennial Parenting Tip!**
> Understand that it may take a little longer than it took you to figure some things out.

My second daughter Jahnique, I'm not sure how her journey is going to end. She is such a beautiful young woman inside and out but a little distracted at times. I'm not sure if she has committed to a career for herself. She has completed a Bachelor's Degree in Psychology, but I don't think she has figured out where to apply it. I love that she is exploring different jobs in the human services field and I know through trial and prayer she will find her niche. I know that she has fulfilled one dream already and that was to be a mom and wife. God blessed her with a beautiful baby boy, and so far, she is doing a great job.

Parent, we know that financial success does not measure dreams, but it is purely the joy of doing something that makes life feel worthwhile, meaningful and purposeful. Dreams are not limited to careers, and our girls will dream of their first kiss, first boyfriend, their college experience, their first all-girls vacation, their wedding, and their first home. They will also dream of their first baby, their first gray hair, their first grandbaby and their 25th wedding anniversary. How will they happen? With time, diligence and constant prayer! Do not give up on yourself or them, you both can have it all.

Here are a few more millennial tips you can share with your daughter.

1. Do not be afraid to pursue your dreams. If your dream is in line with God's will, he will prepare the hearts of the people to receive you.
2. Your dreams do not have to be endorsed by others.
3. Share your dreams with those you trust to nurture them and encourage you along the way.

As for me, my dreams are fulfilled daily. One of which is to make as many people smile as humanly possible, using as many outlets as possible. I believe God anointed me to make people smile. My prayer is that they will see the joy of Lord through me. I have to admit that I have allowed fear to stop me but no more I am going after this dream with all I have.

It Worked For Me...

This subject is very sensitive for so many of our girls. They look in the mirror and don't love who they see. Whether it be the shade of their brown, pimples or a large nose we must help them love the skin they are in and understand that!

1. Brown is brown, and no matter what shade it is, the world will see them as an African American.
2. Puberty is the process, and the pimples will go away!
3. Be proud of their brown skin don't ever let anyone make them feel like they're not good enough.
4. Please put an end to the inner racial complexion issue light skin and dark skin are all brown skin.
5. Loving self and beauty are from inside out. Someone out there will agree.
6. Love has no color, if a person treats you nice, reciprocate.
7. God made us all in his image, so there is no way he meant for us to have a problem with someone that has a different skin color.

YOU ARE NOT YOUR SKIN

I have a question. What would you say if your child looks you in the eyes and says Mommy, why are you white and why am I black? My daughter was so close to tears you could see them at the rims of her eyes. I could not imagine who told her this or made her feel bad about who she was. Shocked, I did not know why she thought I was white. She said to me, "Your skin is so light like the white people and mine is so dark why is that." I said, "baby we are both black, and black comes in many shades. You are the perfect shade of brown." She said, "I want it to be white like you!" As my tears fell, I am wondering why my five-year-old baby was worried about the color of her skin. Who has made her feel inferior and that her color was less than theirs?

I took her to the mirror, and I showed her herself. I told her to tell herself, "Hi Jorri, you are a beautiful brown girl, and God made you in his image. My mommy and daddy love me so much. When they made me, they mixed half of her light skin and half of his dark skin to make me a beautiful shade of brown." I told her you are just perfect the way you are. Until this day I often wonder who told her that she wasn't beautiful brown and why? Sadly, this is the world we currently live in, and we must prepare our babies for these moments.

> **Millennial Parenting Tip!**
> It's never too early or too late to teach our girls how to affirm themselves.

I wonder why black women are so concerned with our shade of black. I have had many darker skin sisters voice their issues with lighter skin women. Many times, they heard that a lighter woman was better than they were. What does that even mean? I have four daughters, two have light brown skin, and two have darker shades of brown. I love them the same, and I thank God there is no divide based on this.

History says that it started in times of slavery with the house Negro the master's kids and the field Negro the not mixed kids. Why wouldn't we seek to free our minds from the shackles of long ago? If you are still festering feelings of inferiority as a darker black woman, let it go, take a deep breath, and release it. You are beautiful, and that's that. To my light skin sisters remember this Black is Black and you are are not special due to the lack of pigment. Let us remember to love each other equally.

The next area of contention for my girls was acne. I had to remind them constantly, whether they had a blemish or a bump, they were beautiful and wonderfully made. I told them to stop looking in the mirror and letting that bump or two control how they felt about themselves. Acne does not define or rule them. Repeatedly, I watched my girls cry because of the breakouts and the monthly bump. You know, puberty, that thing we must endure and take it as a badge of honor to become a young woman.

Here are a few more things I have shared with my girls. Some of these you may know already. However, I encourage you to share these in your own way.

1. Look in the mirror and tell yourself, I am beautiful!
2. Don't let anyone's opinion outweigh the opinion you have for yourself.
3. God will judge your heart and not your face.
4. Outer beauty is temporary, but inner beauty lasts forever.
5. Do not judge others by their skin because there are nice and nasty people who are all colors.
6. Solid relationships are built on what we have in common and not by what we look like.
7. It's okay to have friends who are of a different race.

> **Millennial Parenting Tip!**
> It's important to show your daughter how beautiful she is inside by highlighting those great qualities.

My oldest daughter suffered from self-esteem issues; not quite loving herself the way she should. However, over the years she has learned to accept herself for whom and whose she is. Her confidence is on fire! She has such freedom as she has not conformed to the daily rules of society. Nor does she worry about what I or anyone else is thinking when they see her in her not so desirable clothing. As she tells me, this is how I am comfortable, sorry you don't like it. She was raised to know that God knows her heart and what she does for him is all that will last.

> **Millennial Parenting Tip!**
> Encourage your daughter to find her comfort spot and dwell in it. However, remember that change is also good.

We know there are many shades of brown. No matter the shade, beauty is there. Mothers and daughters we must love ourselves into a comfortable place whether slim, plump, big-boned or overweight, own the skin you are in on a daily basis.

Keep your mind open and your heart too and you will see that we are alike. When you choose who is in your circle, don't allow your skin or theirs to be a factor because we should love people for who they are. We all have to get along as God made us all in His image. If we love Him, we must love all of our brothers, our sisters and color should not have a place in our life. Why? God loves us all the same!

It Worked For Me...

Growing up, I wasn't given direction on sexuality or virginity. I can honestly say I wish someone told what a wonderful gift my virginity was. I have been very boisterous with my girls and not afraid to talk to them. Neither should you be afraid to talk to yours for it can change their lives. It is one of the most important conversations you'll ever have with her. Do not shortchange yourself or her and share.

1. Virginity is the one thing you have more precious than anything you can purchase. Its value is priceless!
2. The difference between foreplay and affection; there is a distinction, and they need to know where and when to draw the line. Your daughter's safety could depend on it.
3. Conversations about virginity, sex, and the freedom to communicate respectfully, letting her know the importance of why you need to speak about it. Do not let some stranger or horny young man do it for you.
4. God says we are to save ourselves for marriage!
5. Sex before graduating from high school is a no, no.
6. Sex is a huge emotional and physical responsibility; give yourself time to grow up!
7. Oral sex is the most intimate form of sex. Don't be fooled into doing it under the premise of still being a virgin.

8. Your first should be someone you foresee spending the rest of your life with. Think hard before taking that step.
9. You are only a virgin once, period and point blank, and no matter of time will make you one again!
10. If you cannot wait, use a condom keep yourself and your future safe!

HOLD UP, WAIT A MINUTE!

In my time of growing up, no one spoke about sex. If they did, it was always with a negative view. I would constantly hear, keep my legs closed, don't be a hoe, don't be nasty and I am sure you can recall a few of your own. What did any of those things have to do with my precious gift that I would one day share with a man that loved and valued me? NOTHING!

I wish someone would have told me to value myself and my body was my temple. I am sure if told this I would have made different choices. I admit that I did not wait but was 15 years old when I had my first experience. I thought it was true love, BUT I can also say he wasn't worth me sharing my body.

> **Millennial Parenting Tip!**
> Be willing to be transparent about your
> first time to prevent mistakes with theirs.

Every parent should saturate their daughter in understanding how valuable they are and that having sex is a huge decision worth waiting until they're truly ready. And, they're more than worth the wait. It may sound simplistic and cliché, but:

1. God says they should wait until marriage.
2. Waiting teaches patience and perseverance.
3. Waiting teaches you the value of you.
4. Once given, virginity cannot be returned or exchanged; it's a final sale.

Parents, we know that this will not be an easy feat to convince them to wait. We also know that temptation will come far more than they could ever imagine, and these young men will try to offer alternatives to penetration, but we need them to know that NO means NO. Tell them about foreplay disguised as affection.

Affection is holding hands, hugging but not frontal rubbing, kissing with your mouth closed and caressing your arms or face vs. foreplay French kissing, touching of breast or buttocks, kissing the neck or lower you get the picture. Teach them that avoidance allows abstinence. There are some clever folks out there, so we need them armed with full armor and knowledge. The ideal goal is to wait until marriage.

Here are a few more tips:

1. Have her imagine the beauty of her wedding night if she waited.
2. Have her sit, really think about and write a list of the qualities the 1st person to touch her body should have.
3. If a single parent, have a brother or uncle share the psychology of boys, what they're looking for, what they will do and say to get what they want.
4. In conversation, respectfully challenge her thoughts of why she believes her choice is worthy of sex.
5. Share the importance of not letting her peers coerce her into having sex to be part of an in-crowd.
6. Teach them about the importance of sexual health and the various STD's and STI's out there.

> Show pictures if you must to bring the point of waiting to their face.
> 7. Don't be as our parents were and not talk about it.

We must encourage our girls to wait and teach them about self-worth. Using the 60-second confession is a good place to talk about waiting. However, instead of them confessing first, you confess something to get your in on the subject. I am happy to report these same principles worked for my older daughters, and they saved themselves until they were mature enough to handle what sex brings.

It Worked For Me...

Dear Parent, having a gay child is not your fault, burden or failure as a parent. She is your child and the entire of who she is, is yours, so embrace it. Apologize if you have made her being gay about you. I had to apologize to my daughter publicly and privately.

1. My daughter being gay has nothing to do with me!
2. It is important to love my child no matter what. The world will be harsh enough.
3. Tolerance is mandatory! We are all different which includes sexual preference.
4. Empower your gay/lesbian child to be all they can be, not act out their gayness if they are. There is no need to practice the part.
5. The word 'Acceptance' means all and not just the parts you like.
6. Tell your daughter that you did not expect them not to love the opposite sex, so please take it easy with you.

You're Gay, But We're Okay

To my daughter, I am sorry! I realized for so long I made you being gay about me. I thought you being gay was a reflection of me and something I did wrong in raising you. I know I was wrong. My hope is after reading this story you will see that I get it and I love you unconditionally. It is ok for you to be gay and I am ok to be the mother of a lesbian daughter. Whew! I said it out loud, that is so liberating.

If you know someone who has a daughter or your daughter is gay, this chapter is just for you. First, once finding out, you probably asked how did this happen to you. Stop right there! It's not about you but this is your child's preference, and she did not choose to be gay to make your life miserable.

As I reflect over the years, I can remember when my daughter was in the first grade, and her school sent home a memo that they would be integrating tolerance for families with gay parents. I was appalled, and I did not want her exposed to that lifestyle. I sent a note to the teacher and told her when you are discussing this I will pick her up, or I want her taken to another class. In hindsight, maybe I should have let her stay. It may have prepared her for her lifestyle because now she is in a relationship with a woman who has a child and it may have been enlightening. I admit that my bias and lack of understanding would not allow it. I don't think I would do it differently because I think first grade was still too much exposure and suggestive. However, I do acknowledge that I could have thought more about tolerance.

> **Millennial Parenting Tip!**
> Do not try to change them. Being gay is not a disease or a condition that will go away with diversion or medication.

I remember when she was a little girl she never liked dolls. I always tried to pique her interest because what little girl doesn't like dolls? Mine! I remember one Christmas I bought Jahnique my size Barbie doll. My thoughts were let me get Jeanette one as well. When she opened that box, she said, "She is not my size!" My daughter never picked up the doll, and that was a $139 lesson.

So many clues come to mind, and I remember when she should've been developing a style of her own. However, she was so tomboyish I thought it was just a phase. I remember we went to a party and one of my cousins pointed to her and said, "Who is that little boy." I was so offended that I wanted to fight her. It was just another clue screaming your baby girl is different. My mind was always screaming she is too young to be gay, but even more so, I kept wondering what I did to make her gay!

My warning to all parents! This lifestyle is hard for our children and they are having a hard time dealing with it. They need you so you are going to have to grow up and deal with it because you could lose them by not wanting to deal with all of them. I said in the beginning

It Worked for Me

that we have to love our whole child even the parts we don't like. So I am sharing so much in this book because I know what I almost lost by not wanting to accept that my daughter was a lesbian.

Jeanette was about 13 or 14 when I came in her room one morning, and she seemed out of it. She told me she took a bottle of Tylenol because life was too hard and she wanted to die. I thought I would die when she said that and hurt she was so desperate for acceptance that she was willing to take her life. I thought to myself; we have to get her help. What can I do to help her? How and who do you go to when your child has attempted to take her own life? How do I prevent her from trying it again?

I can remember the shame I felt as a parent explaining to the psychiatrist that my daughter had attempted to take her own life and I needed help. I remember thinking does she have mental health issues and if so where did they come from.

Millennial Parenting Tip!
Understand that being gay is not genetic but preference.

I made yet another mistake trying to blame other things or even genetics rather than accept my child is Gay! However, I was not so into myself that I could not see that I had to help her. I got her some therapy, which taught her how to cope with her feelings, and she did not make any further attempts at ending her life. To God be the Glory!

I must admit I did not take it to God like I should have because I felt like He did not want to help me with this one. In addition, being gay was one of those sins they talk about on television and radio where God does not accept that lifestyle. Side note I was also a baby in Christ at this time. Looking back, I can see with clarity that God is concerned with everything in my life and that it was His grace and mercy not an ambulance moment when she took those pills. He was watching over her without concern of her sexual preference. He understood that the devil has spirits and that anytime when she is ready, it can be rebuked. Again, I must remind you that your child being gay is not about you. When he or she wants to be openly gay, do not close the closet door. I know you're saying didn't you do that? I sure did, but I want you to learn from my mistakes.

At 16 years old, my daughter threatened to come out of the closet and let the world know that she was gay. Let me tell you I panicked and thought I could not allow her to expose me. I know! Did I just say 'expose me'? Yes, I could not let her tell anyone even though it was quite obvious on sight. However, to verbally acknowledge to our family and friends, what would they think about me? I told her she was free to come out of her room at any time, anything else we need to wait for LOL. I convinced her that if she still felt the same way in five years, then she and I would come out together. Meanwhile, I had my fingers crossed behind my back praying things would change, and she would be straight by then.

I am sharing all of this because I know I am not the only woman who has raised a gay child. I also know

It Worked for Me

that I am not the only one who was ashamed or embarrassed for letting the thoughts of others control the moves we made. I stand on my decision on her coming out at such a young age even though my motives may not have been totally for her. I believe that we all needed time to adjust; she needed to grow up some more and prepare for the judgment that comes with her lifestyle. Mommy had to grow up some as well and realize it was not about her. Go figure, isn't everything about me?

> **Millennial Parenting Tip!**
> You have to get comfortable with letting your daughter be herself.

I think it's valuable to share the perception of my husband's view and how he handled this process. Well, if you ask her, she will say terribly. Then, she will smile and say not as bad as he could have. My husband is an old school soul, but he loves his daughter. I would say he is uncomfortable to let her be herself. He's not happy with her lifestyle, at all, for so many reasons; he had so many expectations for his firstborn. He has always dreamt about chasing away boys coming to pick up his baby and to walk her down the aisle to her husband. In his mind, none of this will happen. He loves this girl with all he has; he is scared that others will not accept and may even hurt her. He knows women in this lifestyle and they never quite found happiness. He just wants her to be happy. Remember this is daddy's first baby girl. However, even with his strong views on this matter, he has never embarrassed her in front of her friends, disowned her or made her choose between the lifestyle and him.

I often had to remind her that I know some of her friends' stories are a lot different. Some came out and could not go back home. Some of their dads have disowned them, and the rest of the family followed. I have prayed for their relationship and that they both would be open to seeing each other's view. Also, I can testify that he does not allow her lifestyle to affect his treatment of her. He would sacrifice his last for her as he would for his other girls. I cannot say that they are currently besties, but I can say that they have mutual respect and have come a long way from where they were. For that, I am grateful. I pray daily for their relationship and for me to stay out of it. They need each other and God to survive.

As for entire household and me, we understand and respect my daughter's lifestyle choice. I just tell her to respect us as well because it is not all about her, LOL.

I cannot close without addressing one of the things that she and I butt heads about; the way she dresses and carries herself. I am always screaming you do not have to wear your gayness. I understand you are who you are but really! I know you think that I don't accept it all if I do not allow her to express herself with her style of dress. However, allow me to explain. If she were into S&M, I would be telling her not to wear her whips and chains outside, so, the same is for this fem and stud thing. If a woman loves a woman, why does she need to look like a man for her to be attractive to another woman? Moreover, if you are a woman who does not like men, why look like one?

It Worked for Me

This world will judge you by how you look, so don't kid yourself. It does not matter what your credentials are or how articulate you may be; they will not get that far because your outer appearance will stop them from talking to you or possibly affording you the opportunity to work for or with them. So I am just saying do not let your appearance speak things for you, let you speak for you, do not rob yourself of the opportunity by thinking they need to accept you as you are. Go figure; I am saying you can look like a woman and be whoever you want to be in your bedroom.

So I know you are wondering where are we now? Me too! LOL. Well, she has the love and respect of all of her sisters. They have their own thing going, and that is truly a blessing. As for my husband, he still grumbles from time to time but he loves his daughter, and that will never change. I am the mother of a Lesbian Daughter, and that is that. Now, I want you to say it aloud. I am the mother of a Lesbian Daughter, and that is that! We have let go and let God.

It Worked For Me...

What you're about to read is a touchy subject but one we must address. So many of us are suffering and have no one or no place to take the pain. I share because I let go, let God, He has healed me, and I hope someone else will receive healing. I would like to think that my daughters are better for it as we have no closed doors. They are open to bringing everything to the table.

1. For every test we have there is a testimony to share.
2. Forgiveness starts within. Once you forgive yourself, you can then forgive others.
3. Don't give anyone or thing a permanent position in your mental stability.
4. Be an advocate for your child, hear them, and acknowledge their pain. Doing this may be the only way they can walk in freedom.
5. Do not give up if the people you trust let you down; they are only human.
6. Pick up your cross and take it to the Lord in prayer.
7. Let go and let God!

Don't Touch Me!

As a mother, I cannot write a book that would talk to so many of life's lessons without sharing one that so many women and men have experienced. I am talking about the inappropriate touch or moment. I am grateful that my experience wasn't as horrific as some, but it left me feeling a way. Most of all if sharing this story helps one person then it was worth bearing my soul to you all.

> **Millennial Parenting Tip!**
> Be willing to appropriately share the bad and the good. Be mindful that sharing is also a way of protecting your daughter.

I am going to share something that I have told very few. When I was about 15, I woke up out of my sleep to see my mother's old man standing in front of me butt naked. I have no idea why I opened my eyes and shut them praying that he would go away. I thank God he did. When my mother found out she initially wanted to defend him and said he was coming from the bathroom. I asked her, "Why did he stop and stare if he was just passing through?" She just gaffed it off as nothing and dismissed me. Devastated, because my mom was a hell-raiser, and she talked a good game. I thought she would have cut his ass to pieces. But nope, she did something I never expected; she simply closed the doors between our rooms and told me to lock my door at night. I could not believe it! I locked my door and slept with a knife under my pillow for at least a year. What the hell is going on? My mom was my hero who fought everyone about everything and the one time I needed her to be my voice she was silent.

Over the years after this experience, I was exposed to many of my sister's boyfriends who thought it was ok to expose themselves, touch me inappropriately, or just say things they should not say to me. I took so much of this abuse because my mom gave me no indication she was on my side or that she was going to do anything about it. I am asking you to listen to your child. They need you to validate their feelings and to stand up for them. You have no idea what they will settle for because the one they depended on let them down.

Now as I sit here a grown woman I can say, Mommy, I forgive you even though you have gone on to glory. It feels good for me to release you and me. I am not giving her a pass or cosigning her lack of action; I am simply saying I understand. My mom was so strong that at times I forgot she was a woman who had needs and weaknesses. She birthed five children, and she took me in as her own when my biological mother passed. She made due with very little, and we always had what we needed. I think that she just wanted to keep her boyfriend for herself even though he wasn't hers to have. Oops, I forgot to mention he was married. Now you may be thinking what in the world was going on. So many levels of dysfunction but in the dynamic of families, there is always a whole lot of bad choices and wrongdoings in the name of love. We are all human, and we all have needs. We all make choices in a moment that we do not think will have such long-term

It Worked for Me

consequences. I have had many trust issues over the years, but if I can help someone let go a lot sooner mission accomplished.

As a parent, perhaps you have sat in judgment of your mother without understanding that back then, and even now parenting has no rulebook to guide us when certain situations come up. Because there is no Chapter 7 in parenting, she did her best to rely on her own experiences, maternal instincts, and prayer. Therefore, let her and yourself off the hook. Let go and let God he will give you peace that surpasses all understanding.

I have been very selective, but have given my girls much advice on how to protect themselves in a situation like this so they would know how to handle themselves when dating or in the company of men. Many have called me the mama bear. I don't play when it comes to my cubs so how did one of my girls experience a sexual incident.

> **Millennial Parenting Tip!**
> Sadly, we live in a culture where assault on young women is rampant. Arm your daughter with the proper tools to defend herself mentally and physically.

Let's fast forward, I have told my children in many ways and so many times do not go to a boy's house without my permission. Also, make sure someone else is in the house at the time they are visiting. If they get there and the person says the mother just went to the store, do not go inside the house. What does my baby girl do? She goes in.

I've told her often that boys think with two heads and the smaller of the two usually rules. When you go into his house with no supervision, the little head comes up with a lot of ideas on what to do.

She was there; no one heard her protesting because she wanted to please him, so she allowed him to kiss her. However, his little head decided she wanted more, and his big head comes up with the idea of what should happen next. She tells him that she doesn't want to partake in his idea. Thank God, he didn't rape her, but he did put his hands in places she did not want. She felt violated, and of course, she did not tell me for weeks after it happened. Of course, I wanted to let her dad loose on the boy, but by this time, her story was fuzzy, and her guilt was strong. We had to talk and pray through this because mentally she wasn't prepared for anything else.

The take away from this is that she was able to trust me through it and I gave her a choice on how we would deal with cementing her trust to bring up future issues. Between my daughter and I, we acknowledged that she did not handle things the way we should have. She was supposed to come home and tell me right away so we could address his behavior. However she didn't want that, so it wasn't done. Was it the right way to handle it, I say absolutely because she had options and she made a choice. Was it the way I wanted to handle it? Not! But as a parent, I felt I had to give her an option because not everyone can handle everything. I was more concerned with her mental health than anything else.

It Worked for Me

> **Millennial Parenting Tip!**
> Make your house a safe haven for your daughter to share with you and her siblings.

I have heard from her sisters that she is very vocal with them about going to boys houses or being alone with a boy. I guess she is using her experience to protect them and at the same time regaining her power. It all worked out in the wash, as I like to say. The lesson to learn for me was sometimes I need to let my girls work some things out for them. I'm not in control of everything. You and I must believe God that you have given them the tools to work it out. Here are a few more tips on how to deal with them sharing an uncomfortable situation of being touched. You have probably heard some of these, but they are worth repeating.

1. At all costs, make them feel safe.
2. Do not choose a stranger over your child.
3. Seek outside help for their healing if necessary.
4. Be in constant prayer for their restoration.
5. If you have some unresolved issues of inappropriate touching, deal with it so you can maturely deal with your daughter.

Of course, we don't want to scare our daughters, but keeping them informed of the culture we live in is important. Moreover, it is equally important to teach them how to protect themselves.

It Worked for Me...

I am my Sister's Keeper! Raised to love other women as I love myself, I encourage women to be all they can be because when my sister wins, so do I. Sadly, people teach others to betray, and we hurt each other for little or nothing. Women, we all have something to offer so let's share our gifts, encourage one another and most importantly, cover one another.

1. Do not audition for another woman's position in her relationship.
2. Do not covet your neighbor's husband.
3. Love your sister who is not your competition, but your friend.
4. Encourage your sister! When she wins, you win.
5. There is always room at the top for both the both of us.
6. Never measure another woman's success by your failure.
7. Love all of your sisters with no limits or barriers.
8. Please do not accept any man's scraps you were born to be #1.
9. Loving other women will help build your character.
10. Imitation is the purest form of flattery if it worked for her it might work for you.
11. There is no shame in seeking direction or mentoring from a woman who has herself together.
12. Remember, we are all individuals with unique gifts.

13. Always give credit where credit is due.
14. Women Rock! Regardless of what anyone says, we have made wonderful contributions to this world.

My Sister's Keeper

Reader, this is going to be the longest chapter in the book because I have so much to say about this topic. I was born to Jeanette and Randolph who have both preceded this book in death. Raised by my mom's sister Georgette who had five kids of her own, I am a self-proclaimed sister's keeper.

I know my aunt could have chosen to send me to live with my dad or his family, but instead, she loved me and kept me for herself. I can hear her now ain't nobody taking my baby nowhere. She let me see my dad but only for a few hours and occasionally for a few days. She sowed good seed in us that we must always love and protect each other and gave a solid example by her relationships with her sister-friends. I just know that I hold sacred every relationship with other women I have had over the years. It is important to me how I treat another sister the way I would like to be treated is the beginning and ending for me.

I am the baby of this bunch and trust me they do not let me forget! I didn't have to experience a lot of things as I watched my sister's burn their hands and hearts. Many times, I came to understand their pain without the firsthand experience. We have had our moments over the years, and there were times when I felt so alone. However, I realized that during those times, they had not abandoned me, but God had separated me as He had some things to show me and I had to grow into my own.

> **Millennial Parenting Tip!**
> Teach your daughter that learning by example is good so they won't have to go down the same path of being hurt.

In this journey called life, there will be times to live, love and laugh but some sisters forget to tell you about the crying. My sisters and I have not always been on the same page. We are like many families who love each other every day but do not like each other sometimes. However, I can tell you that you had better not send for one of us because all of us will come for you. I thought of sharing some stories of my childhood and the pain that was in them, but I think some things are left better unsaid because my God told me to let go and let Him. For that, I am grateful, and His peace is like no other. I want to walk forward and if I stumble back and thank God for the moment.

> **Millennial Parenting Tip!**
> Teach your daughters to thank God for the lessons learned early on.

I raised my girls to be their sister's keeper and have been adamant that they support each other. I have never fostered any nonsense between them. I have taught them that they are all individuals with their own personalities and to love each other for who they are. The older two keep each other's secrets; they love to laugh when they confess the things they did. I always get the last laugh when I tell them that I was always praying for a hedge of protection all around them. I have had my moments with those two, but they came to understand that I was not playing if they did not get along with each other.

> **Millennial Parenting Tip!**
> Teach your daughters if they can't get along with each other, it will be hard to get along with other women.

When they were younger and would bicker, I would make them stand in the corner and hug each other until they both walked away smiling. My girls knew whatever the issue was better be worked out or I would shut them down with no outside company at all. They hated it but have learned the importance of having each other's back.

Now, the last two are quite a job and bicker constantly. The difference in age is the biggest of the problem one is 19 and the other 15, so you know miss 15 wants to be an equal. I am constantly shutting them down, but as I write this, I think they may need to get in the corner and hug.

The main thing I want them to understand is one of the best relationships you have should is with your siblings; love them, respect your differences, and forgive each other. We all will make a mistake, and it's ok to forgive and let it go. Sisters are your memory keepers they are the ones that see it all. When you need to laugh at yourself or cry with someone, they will always be there.

It Worked for Me

Remember when someone brings you a grievance, please honor it and do not take the attitude that they're petty because we all have different petty meters. Sisters and brothers bring your grievances, stop holding on forever never telling the person what they did to offend you. Not sharing turns into years of time wasted. Reader, if you are presented with a situation *'always'* check yourself. Examine what you did or said and if you were wrong, apologize even if you cannot see your wrong in the situation. Still, apologize for the pain it caused them and move on. If they cannot move on, then *'pray'* for them. I want you to understand that life is way too short to stay stuck letting one day, one year or ten years go by without speaking to someone. It is ridiculous and not worth the moment's loss.

I must discuss the sisters we inherit along life's journey, the women who come in your life and love you harder, deeper and sweeter than any of your natural sisters. I call them my sister-friends chosen for each other handpicked by God. They will come in your life, but some come for a reason so do not try to hold them longer than their purpose. Some sisters come for a season; they too had a purpose, their time, and they knew exactly what you needed. Thank God for them all! However, mostly there are those who were sent to be with us forever and those are the ones you cherish because they will understand you.

Millennial Parent Tip!
We can't just say but must show our girls
to not have loose morals!

This world emulates so many things we shouldn't like, television shows that have the president's side piece glorified and a newscaster thotafied, this is what so many of our girls are idolizing. Parents, we must remind our girls of a few things:

1. Do not backbite or plot on your sister or what's hers.
2. When you smile at her as she walks by, do not whisper mean things when she is no longer present.
3. If a man has a wife, girlfriend or boo, you do not want him. He is not available!
4. Consider another woman's feeling because karma is powerful and very real.
5. Never practice trying to be someone other than yourself.
6. Despite what they see on television, self-worth is more important than anything.

Don't be a hater! Be a congratulator! You never win because she loses, and never forget that. Celebrate her victories as if they were yours. We are all destined to do great things, effort and faith will get you there. Her success is not your failure you are a winner always! Remind yourself that you can have anything you want if you work hard and stay the course.

> **Millennial Parenting Tip!**
> Teach your daughters to never sit
> and wait for another woman to fail.

God blesses us all in different areas, trust me if you sat around the table with the most beautiful women in the world and heard their stories you would gladly take your problems and run home. Here are a few more things to share:

1. Do not let the world tell you what beautiful looks like; I want your mirror to tell you.
2. Be approachable, loving and genuine, and you will see that beauty lives inside of you.
3. Remember all that glitters isn't gold.
4. Be a cheerleader for others but most importantly, yourself.

> **Millennial Parenting Tip!**
> Encourage your daughters to write and recite to each other... I am beautiful! I am worthy! I am a child of God!

To all my sister-friends, I love you all! GOD has been kind enough to send me some wonderful women to call my friends, and I value the sisterhood. You ladies saw me through so many moments, high and low. We have to stay friends forever because you have been my secret keepers. I have never wanted anything less for you than I wanted for myself. We have encouraged, uplifted, undergirded and prayed for each other. I am glad for the times we share, could not share because of being embarrassed but you knew anyway, I am most grateful for our sister love. We are truly each other's keeper!

    I hope I have shown my girls an example of what a sister should do and I hope they will carry this on. I could not end this without leaving you with a few women that I consider ones to watch. As you should already know I am a lover of women, I know that we rock! I am going to introduce to you some women I believe are worth watching and emulating, these girls are some real SHEROES!

First, there was Mary; she was the mother of Jesus who can teach you about sacrifice and obedience. Imagine you are a teenager, a virgin and are pregnant and God tells you that your husband will be a 90 something-year-old man. Pause and think isn't that something to handle as a young woman? Now think about the adolescent issues you had, I bet you couldn't handle what she did. I do want you to learn from her story that faith in God's word, when unwavering, will reap blessings that you cannot imagine. You may not be the mother of the Messiah, our Lord, and Savior Jesus, but you can give birth to new ideas, inventions, cures and solutions that can change the world.

Then there is Esther, a woman of character and honor but also knew how to keep her mouth shut. She was the wife of the King Ahasuerus when she learned that the king's right-hand man was going to kill her people. She was smart and never told anyone who her people were. When her cousin Mordecai came to tell her that she was her peoples only hope, she devised a plan. She went before her husband unannounced, which could have meant death. But she persevered, invited the king and the enemy Haman for dinner and she won the king's favor. When she told the king that Haman was planning on killing her family the king had him killed. You must know how to play your position to

It Worked for Me

get what you want while understanding your environment.

Let's meet Naomi's daughter in law Ruth who could have abandoned her mother in law like her sister in law did after the death of their husbands. But instead, she stayed. For this, she received reward, favor, married Boaz, and many generational blessings. The moral of the story is, don't be a fair-weather friend only with people when they are up, but at the first sign of trouble, you are out. Instead, learn how to weather the storm, stand beside your people, and let God get the glory with the wonderful story.

I gave you some historical women, they all lived either while Jesus was here or before. These examples of characters that God chose to share in our most sacred book, the Bible. No doubt, that was just a few, but God gave us many, as He knew we would need examples.

Let's talk about some women we see every day who are living their truths right in front of us. I want to tell you about some everyday sister's that can help you become a better woman. There are many women of color on television with attractive qualities. We should look and learn a few things without trying to be them. Take what you need and leave the rest. Whatever we do, we must teach our girls not to get caught up in acting black, a stereotype we need to drop it where it was picked it up.

Our first African American first lady Michelle Obama is a strong black woman who was ordained to be our first lady of color. Not many of us have the poise, the keen ability to observe, and know not to react, listen and not argue. She will tell you she grew up like many of us with very humble beginnings, but what she did differently was take advantage of all the opportunities that came her way. From being committed to her studies and believing in herself she knew that she could achieve all things through Christ that strengthens me and you. I watch her so often have to bite her tongue when the nasty folks called reporters were throwing everything they could at her. She simply smiled and said "When they go low we go high'. She did not roll her eyes, neck or cuss she just simply smiled and moved on. Mrs. Obama is a woman to watch and emulate. Her character is strong, but I believe her faith was stronger.

I have a girlfriend, her name is Clara, and she will probably cry a little when she reads this, but she is one of my sheroes. She had a very humble beginning growing up in a housing development in Queens, but she never let that become her. She married her teenage crush, and she became a teenage mom. She broke a cycle of being what people call "the baby momma." She could have let her circumstances write the book about her future instead she was poised, smart, stood back, and observed the rules and game of the banking business. She started as a teller in the bank, but she did not stay long, she took advantage of opportunities, and she is now a Vice President at one of the major banks and accomplished this by 40. Not only did she do that, but she also encouraged her daughters to be better educated, and in the process of raising them, she decided she would too. Clara went back to school and went all the way up to earning her Master's Degree. She did that while holding down a job, husband, children and a home and did not miss a beat. Mothers, I want you to remember it is never too late and there is nothing you cannot be. Clara did not let the stereotypes keep her a bank teller, or let her be a single mom or let her live in the projects as if it was a birthright. She broke so many chains, and for that, I applaud her. Clara, I love you, and you inspire me!

My first lady is wow! She is a woman of God whose strength is unparalleled. Young ladies, if you want to see a woman of God in action here, she is! When I say, someone is ordained to be a first lady my sister here is that. She has mastered how to bless you even when you try to curse her, and that is what I admire most. Her strength is quiet but loud at the same time. She does not raise her voice or roll her neck but simply says what it is and moves on. She supports her husband and his vision and does not let the devil make her lose focus. By watching her and participating in her Sisterhood ministry, she has taught me a lot as a woman like how to have a better prayer life, how to keep God in my thoughts and how to go to Him before I make decisions.

Millennial Parenting Tip!
Teach your daughter's the power of praying before talking.

She teaches that prayer is a great help for the wife, worker, mother and most of all a sister. Kindness is what you see, and a change of atmosphere is what you will get when she enters a room. I salute you my sister, my friend, and mentor for all your roles and all the hats you must wear. You are doing a great job, and I am sure our Heavenly Father is well pleased with you.

My sister in love Alisa she is a wife and personifies the qualities that make a good wife. She is kind, patient, loyal, faithful and loving. She took her vows seriously; I would say her parents were her example of a strong marriage and it was death that did them part. Alisa, I watched you go from high to low without complaining (a lot) or packing up or throwing in the towel. I was not in your home, so I don't know the struggle, but I know that you came out unscathed, your outer glow is still there, and your smile is still bright. I cannot thank you enough for loving my brother and raising my nieces to be strong young women who aren't afraid to take their own paths. You most certainly are one to watch!

Now for the sisters that either have lost a child or never had a child, but they have used those maternal instincts to make the lives of other people's children that much better. To my very own sissy Rhonda, an amazing woman who has embraced her nieces, nephews and everyone's baby with love that only a mother would understand. She has given tirelessly to her family sometimes without a thought for herself. Just know sis, I love you and thank God for your heart, my babies are better for it.

I see you Beverly J. and Cynthia E. nurturing babies that did not come from your womb, but being so impactful into their lives. Beverly, your scholarship ministry over the years, has grown strong. God had a calling on your life, you took it, ran, and for that I commend you. Cynthia you never stop loving and taking care of those babies that came into your home on that fateful day. Even when the odds were stacked against you and folks tried, you never wavered from being you or loving those babies. These women could be bitter, but instead, they are better. I salute you! I bet you never knew how I saw you. Love you ladies!!

So many women in my life and in yours help us to be stronger, wiser and better. So, remember we all have a story, but we must give God the glory always. I commend you all, for my life would not be the same without you. Our daughters will be better because they have great women to watch and learn from, so ladies, keep your torches on!

Now that I have shared the importance of being your sister's keeper, I cannot go on in this book without speaking of the things I am seeing with so many young ladies these days. It appears, there is a side to the millennial generation that welcomes violence toward each other. Bullying, posting fight videos, jealousy, public shaming, and the list goes on. In recent months, we saw the story of a young girl who was attacked in the bathroom at school and hit her head on the side of the sink, which resulted in her death. And, in recent weeks, the young lady who went out with her friends and the alleged story is they were paid a few hundred bucks to bring her to a party for a scheduled sexual assault. The young lady was later found dead in a freezer.

The question is how do we as parents work harder to protect and ensure our children are not going down the wrong path. How can we show them that being a sister's keeper is not just the person in your family but girls and young women in general? I have a few suggestions.

1. First, understand that we are not animals and are not meant to fight.
2. If your child likes to fight, have them learn some discipline and join a sport such as boxing, wrestling or karate to channel that energy.
3. Stop encouraging our children to fight, period. There is no hood trophy for being the champion of the block.
4. Do not allow your girls to watch video fights and share them with others on social media. Sharing only encourages a behavior we should be rejecting.
5. Daily teach consequences for actions like sharing articles and information of girls their age who suffered serious repercussions for their actions.
6. Daily teach your girls not to follow behind a crazy friend and be a leader.
7. Teach our girls problem-solving skills so they can navigate their journey looking for resolutions that do not include violence.
8. When you spot the spirit of anger ask them why they're so angry? Their aggression came from somewhere.
9. Constantly, work to expose them to the positive like young entrepreneurs, positive girl groups or others their age doing great things. Letting them know that they can do great things as well if they choose the correct path.
10. Most importantly, telling them in love that God is not pleased with their behavior.

We must constantly work together as parents and caretakers to evaluate the plans for our girls. Are we encouraging our kids to be leaders or followers? Are we raising warriors or intelligent young women? For all of this to stop, it must start with us women who are seasoned and have a passion for reaching our girls.

It Worked For Me...

I want to speak to the saying there is 'death' and 'life' in the tongue because it is true. That little muscle is stronger than any bodybuilder is for it can tear things down or build them up, what will you choose to do with that little member? Consider this:

1. Choosing to speak life into everything dead in your life.
2. What you say has just as an effect on your child as what you do.
3. Not being known as the one whom constantly uses their tongue as a taser.
4. If you have nothing nice to say opt not to say anything.
5. Having a kind conversation and not walking around ripping people to shreds.
6. Being careful about what you put in the atmosphere it may become your reality.
7. Speaking truth but remembering not everyone is ready; not using your words to be destructive. i.e., Girl, you are putting on some weight!
8. No negativity or carrying the name Debbie Downer!
9. Changing your atmosphere to a positive one, especially, when you walk into a room!

DON'T LET YOUR TONGUE BE A TASER

"This you know, my beloved brethren. But everyone must be quick to hear and slow to speak and slow to anger."

–James 1:19

> **Millennial Parenting Tip!**
> Sticks and stone may break my bones, but words will never hurt me this is the biggest story ever told.

I bet you can agree that you don't remember your injuries or even a butt whooping like you remember the unkind words said by your parents, teachers, siblings, relatives, and friends. Once the words are said, you cannot take them back from the person who heard them.

Ladies we must learn to fight fair for we have that lecherous tongue which sometimes fills our mouths with ugly vocabulary. Love is kind, it does not search to hurt, nor does it look to cause pain. If we want to be in a relationship, we will need to control our tongues and emotions.

I have learned that how you say something will affect the atmosphere just as much as what you say. We do not want to be the neck roller always spewing negativity looking to make something out of nothing. Who would want to be around that? The best advice I can give is when you have nothing nice to say then say nothing. Put a positive spin on things, do not contribute to a fire, or bring more hot air to keep the fire-breathing, but bring the water to put it out. No gossiping or you will find yourself in the middle of things all the time and eventually become *the* gossip.

You have the power to speak things in your life good and bad, choose to speak good things like success, having a healthy family, the future, dreams, aspirations, faith and most importantly, God. Your conversation will tell a lot about you if you never have kind things to say.

I had to check myself with my kids. There were times when my girls would sass me, and I would ask, "Who do you think you are?" They would put their little heads down and say "Nobody!" Was I looking for that answer? Absolutely not, but it's what I said when I told them you're nobody up in here. Was it a planted seed I wanted to grow? No! I immediately fixed that I told them when anybody asks who they were; their answer should be "I am the child of the most high GOD!" I also started to speak things into their lives, setting goals, praising them, encouraging them and then I slowly started hearing them speak things into their own lives.

My youngest Jalena has a vision board on her wall right now with quotes to encourage herself. Some of the quotes are I am strong, live, love and laugh, pretty is as pretty does, I am beautiful, no regrets just love, I am fearless, I am wise and don't let anyone stop you from being the best person you can be. I am so proud of her speaking all of this positive energy, and the best thing is that I have used those words to encourage myself some days.

I watch my daughter Jahnique with her son, and she speaks kindly to him with much love and hopes that I tear up sometimes. I know that God is working through her to make her son into a strong and humble man. She calls him a Prince, a title that will make him think of royal things and a name that comes with responsibility.

> **Millennial Parenting Tip!**
> You have the type of power in your tongue
> that can change your family.

We must teach our daughter to speak kindness, love, patience, positivity, beauty and never defeat. We want them to have a great reputation for being respectful and gentle with their words. If we teach them this now, we are preparing them for better relationships and ultimately marriage.

It Worked For Me...

I'm a strong believer in instruction and the need for it! We cannot fail to tell our children things because we're uncomfortable talking about it. The better you prepare your child, the better decisions they will make. I have given my daughters the best advice I could on dating and marriage because I know that it's a very hot topic for young women. However, I do wish that dating be outlawed until their about 30 years old. LOL... So, here it goes.

1. You have to deal with dating like every area of your child's growth with much thought and consideration. Their curiosity will not go away just because you don't address it.
2. Set a rule and then watch them break it! Yes, you read correctly. You and I can have a sidebar conversation about this one.
3. Control is key, but compromise will rule. Be smart; you were a teenager once yourself.
4. Once your child believes you are not compromising with them, they will rebel.
5. Dating is a part of the human experience; we were born to mate, it is our instinct.
6. Take control of what your child knows and understands about their sexuality and behavior; if you don't do it, someone, else will.
7. Relax and talk to your kids. They have a lot of pressure on them from social media, friends and potential boy/girlfriends. You want to prepare them for potential scenarios.

8. Please tell them the difference between affection and foreplay; it may save the day for them.
9. When a man finds a wife, he finds a good thing! This saying is still true!
10. If he disrespects his mom your next, we know this statement to be true!
11. If a man loves and respects his mom, he will do the same to you.
12. Never encourage a rift between any man and his mom. Believe me; it won't end well for you!
13. A man should show you certain things before he is a candidate for any serious dating, and especially, to be your husband.
14. No one man or woman comes into your life to make you happy; they come to make you happier. Do not forget that you are the only one responsible for your happiness.

DATING – LAUGHING OUT LOUD

"A man's courting of a woman, seeking the affections of a woman usually with the hope of marriage" is the dictionary definition of "Courting."

Parents, this is a subject that we can agree makes us cringe and want to run and hide. Well, the 21-year-old mother in me said that my daughters would not date until they are 16. No exceptions to that! I said it, and I meant. As the saying goes if you want to give God a laugh, tell Him your plans.

As my girls grew up, I realized that ha-ha Monique you will bend and compromise because the heart wants what the heart wants and the teenager wants what she wants. So, here is what I did.

When the oldest one first came to me at age 15 and said she wanted to go on a date with the boy from the band, now remember she is the gay, so I was like yes Monique, you can throw that 16 rule right out the window. I took photos and everything. I share this because you will compromise and laugh, but most of all, you will stay in control.

> **Millennial Parenting Tip!**
> Each daughter is different and will mature differently.

Some girls are boy crazy, some are sneaky, and some are creative in how they get their way when it comes to dating. You must identify their strengths and weaknesses, but most of all, strategize. Never let them see

It Worked for Me

you sweat and stay in control of the situation. A parent compromising is not a weakness for our daughters are people too and deserve consideration. And my motto was, compromise now, so I don't have to cry later.

I can remember the many fun times my daughter Jorri, who recorded every infraction to any rule, noticed that her older sister did not have a boyfriend. So, Jorri decided she would go on the website 'Black People Meet' and start a profile. Now my older daughter who is gay and her little sister who is unaware she's gay says, "Hey sis, got you a match a nice young man in Uniondale he is blah blah..." We cracked up in laughter. This 13-year-old girl is setting up profiles and where did she learn about dating websites. Talk about an eye-opener! I had to make sure she did not have one for herself, but she was so sweet and said, "No mommy I just want to get my sister a husband she is getting old." I said right there she is her sister's keeper.

Jahnique was always a little creative; she put me on to group dating. The first two times I didn't realize the amount of boy's and girl's names were equal. She fooled me once, but I checked her twice. We came to understand that I was not slow and knew there were as many girls as boys. What Ms. Jahnique, was doing was dating and if she wanted to go the young man must come to my door. She got it, and we had no further issues. However, she did think that I was so embarrassing. LOL!

Jorri was always concerned with dating because she was always taller than the boys and felt like no one liked her. When I noticed that a young man was showing interest, she was quite excited, and she kept talking about them hanging out.

> **Millennial Parenting Tip!**
> There's nothing wrong with the old fashioned way. Be a chaperone to stay aware and in control of a dating situation.

I saw all the warning signs to say no, and she would still go, so I kept my eyes on the situation. I allowed him to come over, sit in the living room, and watch television. I took them to a movie, so she got what she wanted, and I got to keep my eyes out. She was fourteen when she had her first male company. We also learned from our bedroom window there was quite a bit of making outdone in our kitchen LOL. You can't stop nature, but you can educate them. Gratefully, my girls aren't too boy crazy and have understood they needed to wait.

> **Millennial Parenting Tip!**
> Teach your girls that things can be greater if they wait until later.

Parents stop and think what dating was like for you. Then I want you to ask your daughter what her expectations are. I did just that and was horrified when I found out the thought process. There was no expectation of being escorted to and from a venue nor did the anticipation a date should treat. Of course, the response floored me, but that is where the teaching of expectations and what's mandatory came in.

Fathers, please take the time to talk to your daughters and be a living example in front of them of how a man should treat a woman, for, she needs to know her value. Who better to put her up on the game than her father? It is important to hear from you that she is beautiful and worth more than all the money in the world. She needs to be encouraged not to settle for the pookies of the world but to look for a partner. She needs to know that marriage is not a fairytale but a coming together of two people that have common interests, goals, and love for one another. Tell her the things she needs to know to be a good woman to her man, and she will value those lessons for all her life. Be careful how you talk to her because she will learn to accept whatever you show her as acceptable. As I previously stated, Daddies are our first real boyfriends. We love you so much, and the sunshine rises and sets on you. Of course, this is a blessing and a burden. So be conscious of the responsibility your baby girl needs you.

Most girls want to date, be in a relationship and ultimately get married. That is the proper ending to the perfect story. However, what else can share with your daughters about relationships, dating, and marriage. Although I did not grow up with my father active in my life, I have learned a few things.

1. Stop wondering "why not me?" Real love happens in the time that God wants and allots.
2. Stop asking, "What does she have that make all the boys want her?" A person's popularity doesn't equate to having a good or respectful relationship. You can only see from the outside and have no idea of what is going on otherwise.

3. Remember, you will kiss many frogs but will only make love to one Prince!
4. Introduce a young man to who you are early on so he will know whom you are, where you stand and can make an informed decision on how you both should move forward.
5. The man of your dreams will appreciate your intelligence.
6. The man of your dreams will be proud of your accomplishments and not jealous or ridiculing of them.
7. The man of your dreams will build you up.
8. If he wants to be your husband, he will show you some things you never saw before and make you feel things you never felt before.
9. He respects his mother because if he does not, he will never respect you.
10. He will love you just the way you are.
11. The guy of your dreams will be sensitive to your needs because he cares about what matters to you.
12. Respect is a two-way street, and you need to care about his interests as well.
13. The man of your dreams will want to spend time with you, in public, because you are important to him.
14. The man of your dreams will pray with you? You should want a man who has a spiritual connection and relationship with God.
15. The man of your dreams will have his finances in a good place so that he can meet your needs.
16. Relationships are so much more than the physical.

It Worked for Me

17. The man of your dreams will not lie, cheat or deliberately hurt you. However, we do know that some may slip up. Weigh the case and pray about the situation.
18. The man of your dreams will have values. Be sure to ask him what they are.
19. The man of your dreams will make you feel safe at all times.
20. Respect from a man is deserving and not optional.

Dating, relationships and anything associated with a boy we are never ready for. However, we can laugh at our compromise and teach our girls based on our experiences so they can grow to have meaningful relationships. And, even though I shared all of this, I still think dating should start at the age of 30. LOL...

PART THREE
FOR GIRLS AND WOMEN IN GENERAL – WHAT WORKED FOR ME IN LIFE

It Worked For Me...

I can't tell you who to believe in, but I believe we all need to have a spiritual relationship with God. We need faith to believe in things we cannot touch or see but know in our hearts it's there. That is what my relationship with my God is important. What He has done for me and has allowed me to share with my daughters is priceless. Why is God Important?

1. The Bible tells us to train a child in the way they should go and they shall never depart.
2. A spiritual relationship of faith and hope is what will keep us.
3. When we follow God and His commandments, we are covered and will receive our reward!
4. Science can say what it wants, but the creations of God are present and everywhere.
5. It doesn't matter what you believe in just know we need a spiritual connection to keep our minds regulated. The world is tough and how will you cope if you have no beliefs.
6. God is important! Teach your child about Him early on trust me it will change their lives. God Is Love!
7. Spiritual connections create conviction which creates consciousness!

GOD IS IMPORTANT

"For God so loved the world that he gave his only begotten Son, whosoever believeth in him should not perish but have everlasting life."
—John 3:16

I am a Christian, I love the Lord, and I will never turn back. And, as for my family, we will serve the Lord. His praise will continually be in my mouth for I am a worshipper! I have raised my girls in church and when I slacked they had a praying fire baptized Grammy that picked up the slack. I gave my girls back to God within in the first six months of their birth, as I understood that they were a gift from God. I was obligated to give them back to Him so that He would keep them in His hands. I needed them to develop a prayer life and seek God first in all things so He could direct their paths. I wanted them to understand that God is all they will ever need in this life and the peace He gifts us with surpasses all understanding.

All of my girls are baptized. The Pastor that married us did the older three, but my current pastor baptized Jalena. The beautiful thing is she stood up and told him at ten years old that she was ready. She was the youngest person he ever baptized, and he usually makes the children wait until they are 13. However, she could answer all his questions and confess her acceptance of Jesus Christ as her Lord and Savior. She has always had a relationship with God, as a little girl she would conduct mock church, and that little sister can pray.

It Worked for Me

My daughters Jeanette and Jahnique were away at college, and they joined a Mime ministry, I cried. It confirmed for me that train a child in the way they should go works. They were ministering to others through mime dance and could have been doing anything, but they found a deeper relationship with God. I could not have been more proud or ask for anything more.

When my daughter Jahnique had my grandson, she christened him in a timely fashion just the way I taught her. Even though her husband is Muslim, he was able to step out of his way and understand his boy needed covering. My baby has my grandson in church often, and he is learning to praise the Lord. She understands the importance of a prayer life. Jahnique has had some challenges in her marriage, and she is playing her position as the praying wife understanding that prayer changes things and through God all things are possible.

My oldest daughter Jeanette just moved to Virginia, and I almost died. However, I realized that she is growing up and possibly need to move to further her growth. In the first couple of days, her prayer life changed, and she was forced to depend on God. She knew that He was the only one she could call on that He would direct her. The first week she had found a job and an apartment, and within 30 days God gave all that she left back to her and made her a group home manager. She has met so many folks that want to help her with her goal of opening her own business. She repeatedly gives God the glory understanding who is her help.

My Jorri is working on her relationship with God. She is a baby in Christ; still not sure of her relationship with Him, however, I know that she knows without Him we can do nothing. Her faith is youthful as she is, but I know that she will grow in Christ because in this life you need Him more than anything.

I don't want to get too preachy, but I do want you to understand I love the Lord, and I will never deny it. I can't tell you who to pray to, but I am encouraging you to establish a relationship with the spiritual power you believe. You will need it! There is peace in prayer, meditation or simply communing with the Lord. I can guarantee you that at some point in your life you will need the Lord like oxygen. Yokes (I will get to that as you continue to read) have broken in my life. God made sure I did not develop a taste for any drugs or cigarettes, and I do not have the spirit of a drunkard! God has come into that delivery room four times, and each time He let me go home with a healthy baby. When I had to have surgery, God has gone in the operating room with me, and when it was taking too long for me to wake up, he made sure I came back to my family. When the diagnosis was grim, he turned what the doctor's saw and could not explain in my favor by just making it disappear. When in some storms, God was that umbrella protecting me and has always given me the peace I needed. I cannot explain the peace God gives you; I can only say it is like no other and the reason I can cope.

I smile each day because God has blessed me openly and privately. I know you are probably scratching your head thinking how does he bless you privately. You ever have the devil sitting in a hospital room telling you-you're not going to make it and then the peace of God the Holy Spirit come in and escort the enemy out? Well, I have! You may think I am crazy that's okay because I have that crazy faith. Mercy is present and my understanding of what it means to have a private blessing. The public blessings are easier to identify if you woke up, can move freely, have an able mind, a house, a car, a job you get the picture. It is all His grace and mercy make no mistake.

It was in my prayer time where I questioned what God would have me to do. He spoke to me and said share your thoughts and wisdom for our daughters. It's funny because for years' people have told me that I have wisdom, kindness and a drawing to that is special, and when I speak I drop little gems of wisdom. I guess God was preparing me for this time when I would share them with the world, and that is what gave birth to this book. Believe me when I tell you that "God is Important!"

It Worked for Me….

Death is guaranteed. How prepared we are when loved ones pass away is another thing altogether. The Bible tells us we can go in a twinkling of the eye. Are you prepared and have you prepared your family for when death comes knocking because it will. I have learned a few things related to someone passing.

1. Grief is real!
2. Give flowers while the person can smell them and spread love while the person is alive.
3. Death is certain! God only promised us two things, and that is life and death.
4. There is no barometer for grief and no embarrassment in needing help.
5. Death is sudden or sometimes we're given God's grace to spend precious moments with our loved one to say goodbye.
6. Let your works speak for you! Which means live a life that will say who you were on this earth.
7. Grief and guilt are two separate situations, but they meet sometimes. You will need to deal with them differently.
8. Death means paradise for the Christian that has lived a right life!
9. Suicide is a sin and selfish, please don't take your own life.

WHY DID SHE HAVE TO DIE?

God promised us two things - life and death!

As a parent what is the hardest thing to explain to your child? I believe it's when your loved one has gone to be with God, and you will no longer see them. To look your child in the eyes and see the confusion, pain, and trying to explain the life cycle is hard.

To top that, you must try to put the sudden death of your loved one in perspective. After experiencing a sudden death, I knew I had to address it with my girls and prepare them for mine, their father or grandmother's death, which are all inevitable. Life is precious but death is guaranteed. When it comes, it is permanent, and there are no do-overs or second chances. I want to talk about the realness of death and the grief one experiences when it knocks at your door.

I have experienced death many times in my life, but the one that knocked me off my square was when one of my best friends died. What an experience that was so overwhelming and unbelievable. I want to share the emotions I felt because you will never understand the full extent of grief until a friend, someone who is the same age and considered to be your sister friend dies. So with death comes grief!

Webster defines grief as, "The normal process of reacting to a loss. The loss may be physical (such as a death), social (such as divorce), or occupational (such as a job)." There is no time limit, or specific protocol for grief only steps for the grief process. You have probably heard some of these before, but I would like to share all of them. You never know when you might need to know that they are.

Stage 1: Shock and Denial – I can testify it's definitely what you will feel especially when it's sudden or unexpected. You will not believe how it happened, and most of all, why God let it happen.

Stage 2: Pain and Guilt – Very real emotions that weigh you down especially if you have not talked to that person within a week of their passing. You may feel an overwhelming sense of guilt questioning why you didn't. I want to tell you now that no man knows the day or hour that God will call anyone home. You have no control so accept and let go.

Stage 3: Anger and Bargaining – You may blame others for it happening, but please don't. It's not anyone's fault. This stage of grief wastes energy, and it may cause you further isolation and pain. You might engage in bargaining with God asking him to return your loved one for something you will give up. Don't do that either because it is in vain our God does not work like that.

Stage 4: Depression – Is what you will feel once your mind admits that the person you loved so dear is gone. Depression is a place you cannot dwell for long, is dangerous and cause you long-term problems. It's a real moment, but you must seek the counsel of a professional and pray as your life depends on it. Your loved one does not want you to stay stuck in this place.

Stage 5: Upward Turn – The moment you realize it's real and you are going to have to accept it. Depression better known as darkness will now start to lighten up, and you may feel a little less pain. However, you're not out of the woods, but it is a step in the right direction. You may have sought a therapist or spiritual counselor, and their advice starts to make sense.

Stage 6: Reconstruction and Working Through – You have started to get back into the groove of living to understand that you need to move forward to keep yourself afloat. Depending on the relationship of the person to you and the role they played in your life you may have to start making decisions about how you are going handle things now that they are gone.

Stage 7: Acceptance and Hope – You're almost there and you have told your heart it's okay to let go and that your loved one is okay and with God. You have let them rest in peace and you are going on with the business of life. You have let go, let God, this is where your prayers are answered and where you realize why and how of their passing.

God makes no mistakes and your loved one's time has come; you must say see you later and work on your dash, which is the part that matters the most. What will you do with your life? I wish someone had warned me about death and what it feels like when you lose someone. I wish they'd told me about the indescribable pain you feel that is so real. Please allow me to share the story of when death reached my door.

On New Year's Eve of 2010, I had just come home from church service bringing in the year prayed up and feeling good. I called my bestie several times that night with no answer. My thoughts were, where is she and she better not have gone out without me. I think I had talked to some folks wishing them a Happy New Year and then I put down my phone. I began talking to my hubby then I see a message from a mutual friend saying, call it is very important. I was like God, please I pray nothing has happened to her mom. So I call her, and she tells me the worst news of my life that our friend Boobie had died.

I could not believe it; I was like why would someone say that when she can't be, she wasn't sick or anything. I called her husband, and he answers the phone, but he cannot speak, I can hear him weeping, and I knew it was true. When I say, New Year's Day of 2011 is one of the worst days of my life, all of the life was sucked right out of me. I was in such a state of shock, I could not get myself together and to top everything off it my baby girls birthday. I had to put on my big girl panties and be strong for her at least to take her to dinner. I did not believe it and asked God, how He could let this happen.

My buddy Boobie was my ride or die friend, and I could trust her with any and everything. We carpooled, worked together, shopped, ate, argued and loved each other like sisters. The funny thing was, she shared the same name as my mom. I just couldn't stomach the whole situation. Her funeral was surreal because we were in our forties so how was I burying my best friend? I would drive to work and cry the whole way there. The Marvin Sapp CD "Never Would Have Made It" was on constant replay and helped me get through

It Worked for Me

my time of sorrow. I cried every day for a year on my way to work some mornings and don't know how I made it there because of all the tears. I am ashamed to say that at times I did not want to live without her. I know you are probably saying she was just a girlfriend. She was so much more than just a good friend but a rare gem and confidant. No judgment, always on your side, had your back, thoughtful and absolutely irreplaceable.

I went into a depressed state, and I know the devil was dancing he had one more or so he thought, but my God said take your hands off her. I can remember that it was just after the first year anniversary of her passing, I went to my Pastor and told him about my struggle and how I needed help with my heart breaking daily; all of it was too much. He hugged me and told me it would be all right and we talked about going to grief counseling. He told me God made all kinds of doctors to help his people. Then it happened one morning I was driving and crying, and God said enough, I have watched you cry every day. I am here to tell you that I am the author and finisher of your fate as I was with your friends. Her date was in the book, she had done her work and had to come home. I cried about why I need to talk to her one more time. He said no baby, you will see her again, but not now, but I will tell you this that you must live and accept that death is mine, I promised you only life and death, and you must accept it. I wiped my face, and I must say I felt a lot better. It was as if the switch came on because I knew that. God makes no mistakes. I still cry sometimes, but I realized God was preparing me for the deaths to come.

I shared this story because I won't be here always and I need my girls to understand and respect death. God is the Alpha and Omega, and He promises us life and death. Live this life always working on your dash. Grief has no timeline, but we cannot remain stuck in time, as time is sure to keep moving.

I have lost many people in my life, but none affected me like losing a friend. I think it's more about your own mortality, and I feel like friends are the family we choose, I chose to love her and was not ready to lose her. You can keep the deceased loved ones alive in your heart as long as you remember the good times and share them with others. By you recalling those great times, they never truly die. As I believe as long as someone is calling your name, you will stay alive.

I advise us all to live our lives like every day is the last. No living with regrets and the woulda, coulda or shoulda just did, doing or done. I miss my friend still, and as I am writing this I weep. However, I know I honor our friendship by sharing my memories of her whenever I can. Therefore, I no longer wonder why she had to go. I know she had to be with God and transitioned from my bestie to my angel, as I know she is watching over me.

Before I move on, I must talk to you about the one thing all Christians dread because we believe that suicide is the one sin that God will not forgive. I know all that read this will have mixed opinions, and that is fine, but I think we can all agree that life and death are in the creator's hand and we should not take it into ours. I have had firsthand experience with the awfulness of suicide, and it leaves the survivors in a state of shock and desperation. The unanswered questions and feelings of inadequacy make those left behind feel like they failed and were blind to that person's hurt.

Can you imagine that one of my bride's maids at my wedding, which was the last day I saw her, would take her own life by the time I returned from my honeymoon? Can you imagine the guilt I felt wondering if my happiness caused her so much pain? I know that in my heart, it wasn't that, but can you imagine? I prayed that was not the case. I would like to believe that she was just in so much pain that she just didn't know how to express or deal with it. She will never know how much we did not understand why or what made her so sad. She will never know that when she took her life how much pain we felt from losing her. I can remember thinking how some people can mask their hurt with smiles and the people around them will never know.

I am asking as you are reading this page if you are in a place where you feel this life is not worth living that you seek help immediately from a loved one, clergy or even the various suicide prevention programs. It is not natural to hurt yourself, so do not do it now! I promise you if allow yourself to see another day a change is sure to come.

The purpose for this chapter was simple to give our children some insight into death and the grieving process because one this is for certain death will come. We need to prepare them with the tools to process and accept grief and then move one.

Love you forever Jeanette "Boobie" Nichols.

It Worked For Me...

I believe this is an important topic especially for those of us who are seasoned in age, have a better understanding of how traditions and yokes work, and how to handle them. We cannot carry things that should be left behind, and it's our responsibility to help those younger than us to see that.

1. Remember to encourage youth to be different because being the same is not progress.
2. Traditions are beautiful, sacred, must be maintained and passed down.
3. Encourage others to start a new tradition, be vigilant in keeping it alive and give someone the responsibility of passing it down.

TRADITIONS VS. YOKES

Tradition, by definition, is the transmission of customs or beliefs from generation to generation or the fact of being passed on in a certain way. Yokes by biblical definition are any kind of teaching, written or spoken, handed down from generation to generation or Yokes defined by Webster is a wooden crosspiece that is fastened over the necks of two animals and attached to the plow or cart that they are to pull (noun) rob; mug: (verb)

Please understand the differences between these very important things in your life. Traditions are honored, yokes are broken, and they are sometimes confused because they are similar. Your family may have many traditions that are dear and sacred, that should be followed and preserved. As a society, we have moved away from many traditions that make us who we are as a people. My family was not big on tradition nor did they have a strong sense of family. I did not know what I was missing until I met the Young's.

My husband's family has deep traditions honoring the elders of the family, attending reunions, family trees and without a doubt respecting the name and what and who it stood for. Having pride in your family name meant NOTHING to me! However, the Young's take pride in everything as well as the accomplishments of their ancestors. They instilled in their generations the importance of not tarnishing or bringing embarrassment to the family name. I know for a fact that traditions are lost because many today don't care how their actions will affect the family. Sadly, they overlook all the struggles gone through to accomplish the things already set up for them. When we walk out the door every day we carry our whole family with us and when we do things that are not right we hurt a whole family not just ourselves.

In my family, we have done our best to maintain certain traditions such as sit-down dinners every Sunday. As time has gone by I can admit I have lost this a bit but in writing. However, I have reconnected, and it's ok to lose the way and then find it. We are all in attendance for holiday dinners, everybody's birthday is important and celebrated, we christen our babies as soon as possible as it is a gift from God that must be acknowledged. We all have a relationship with our Lord and Savior.

Now to the good part, the part I love because God is so good that He will break yokes in your life that will not become a tradition or legacy. So how can one overcome a yoke in their family history? The first answer would be to pray and declare deliverance for your bloodline. The second answer would be to do the opposite of what that person in your family did. However, why not go a step further and be proactive in breaking the yoke.

1. Is there a history of drug addiction in the family? Learn alternative ways of healing besides the traditional way of using drugs.
2. Is there an alcoholism addiction in the family? Look up the potential health effects and risks associated with abusing alcohol.

3. Is there a history of financial problems or poverty within your family history? Learn about money, how it can work for you and teach a young person in your family what you have learned.
4. Is there a history of domestic abuse in the family? Learn the blatant and hidden warning signs of abuse. Connect yourself with healthy people and relationships.
5. Is there a history of depression? Talk with a psychologist, even if you are not, to understand what depression is and how one can deal or combat going there.

What am I saying? Education is one of the major keys to breaking yokes. When we are fully informed, it helps in our decision-making process to do better, especially, when we have grown up in certain environments.

We should instill in our children a desire to move and go beyond what we have done. I am so proud of my girls that three out of four have graduated high school all with distinction and the two oldest have graduated from college with their bachelor's degrees and the third is going into her junior year of college. I instilled in them from the beginning that not going to college was not an option and presented as a goal and tradition for our family. Their generation of Young's will all be college graduates, and I have no doubt I will have four for four achieving this goal. I can remember my husband saying that all of his family graduated from high school. My story is a little different, as three out of six of us have graduated high school. I often think how different things would have been if we were encouraged from the beginning that it was not an option not to graduate. Therefore, I stand today thinking one yoke down!

Both my biological parents suffered with substance abuse and by God's grace that has not happened to me. I can testify that yoke has been destroyed, my children don't have those issues and am in constant prayer covering them. Depression has tried to creep on me, but God said not so.

It's important that we recognize traditions versus yokes and rebuke the yokes that destroy our legacy. We must stop excusing and allowing yokes to be a traditional disease in our families. We have control! We can break the YOKE for generations to come.

FINAL THOUGHTS

The idea of writing a book never really crossed my mind because I always thought I would be a comedian. One of my gifts is laughter. But, I prayed to God in a place of desperation seeking his counsel because my life felt purposeless. I do not know you, but I worked at the same job for 20 years with no satisfaction. I had not fulfilled my purpose, so in my praying and crying, I heard God say to me share thoughts concerning our daughters. First, I thought how Lord because boy do I have some thoughts for these young women. Are you sure, you want me to share them all? Then I started hearing it repeatedly, and I realized how I could share thoughts for my daughter and your daughter and our daughter, so I began to write.

    I am an avid reader so I thought it would be easy, NOT. The funny thing is I love romance novels, so this was going to be a stretch. I am used to reading about a hero and heroine so how do I make up a story about my thoughts? However, my heavenly father stepped in again and sent me to my sister in Christ, I told her of my vision, and she paired me with two more sisters that would help carry my vision and not kill it.

    Daughters get some women in your life that will help carry your vision. Do not let the devil come into your life and wreak havoc stopping you from getting where you're destined to be. Remember the enemy comes only to kill, steal, and destroy. You will notice that some folks are so negative they cannot see beyond their nose. Those people only spew venom, and you will have to drop them off along the way. I have had a few women in my life that were dead weight, one day I turned around, and they were gone. No fight or fuss just went, that was God. He will remove folks, and when He does, let them go. Do not go looking for them, don't invite them back in, let them go and let God do what He does.

I hope you received something from reading this book; I know it was very cleansing for me. I didn't realize how many times God had to rescue me and protect me all of this for this moment. Who knew that He would use me to speak to His people, talk about how to raise our daughters, help elevate our young women, and let me share with "What Worked For Me!!!"

The End!

CPSIA information can be obtained
at www.ICGtesting.com
Printed in the USA
FFOW04n2307130418
46262156-47684FF